SISTERS ON THE FLY®

Other Books by Irene Rawlings

The Clothesline

Portable Houses

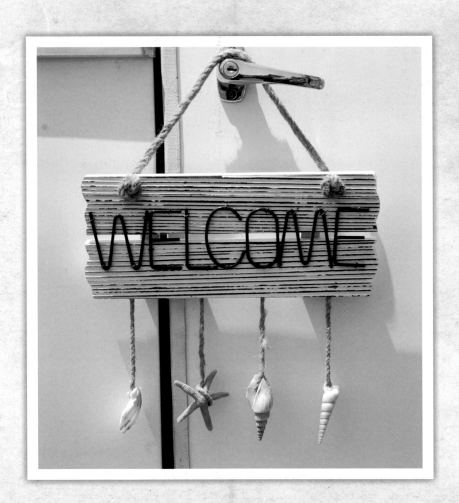

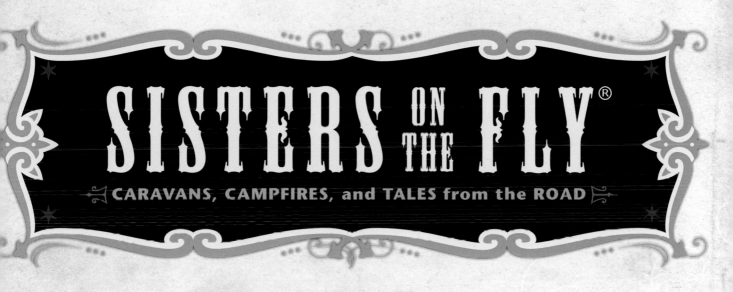

SISTERS ON THE FLY®

CARAVANS, CAMPFIRES, and TALES from the ROAD

IRENE RAWLINGS

Photographs by David Foxhoven
and Audrey Hall

Andrews McMeel
Publishing, LLC
Kansas City • Sydney • London

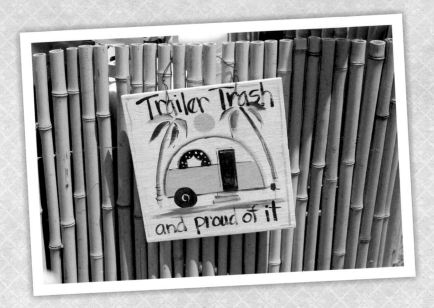

ISBN-13: 978-0-7407-9131-4
ISBN-10: 0-7407-9131-1

Library of Congress Control Number: 2009943087

10 11 12 13 14 WKT 10 9 8 7 6 5 4 3 2 1

www.andrewsmcmeel.com

Book design by Holly Camerlinck

ATTENTION: SCHOOLS AND BUSINESSES
Andrews McMeel books are available at quantity discounts with bulk purchase for educational, business, or sales promotional use. For information, please write to: Special Sales Department, Andrews McMeel Publishing, LLC, 1130 Walnut Street, Kansas City, Missouri 64106.

For the amazing Mazie. We all want to be just like you!

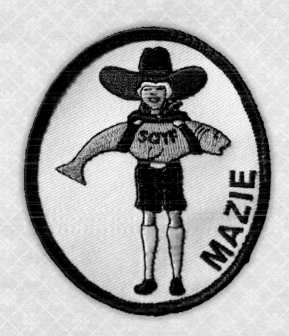

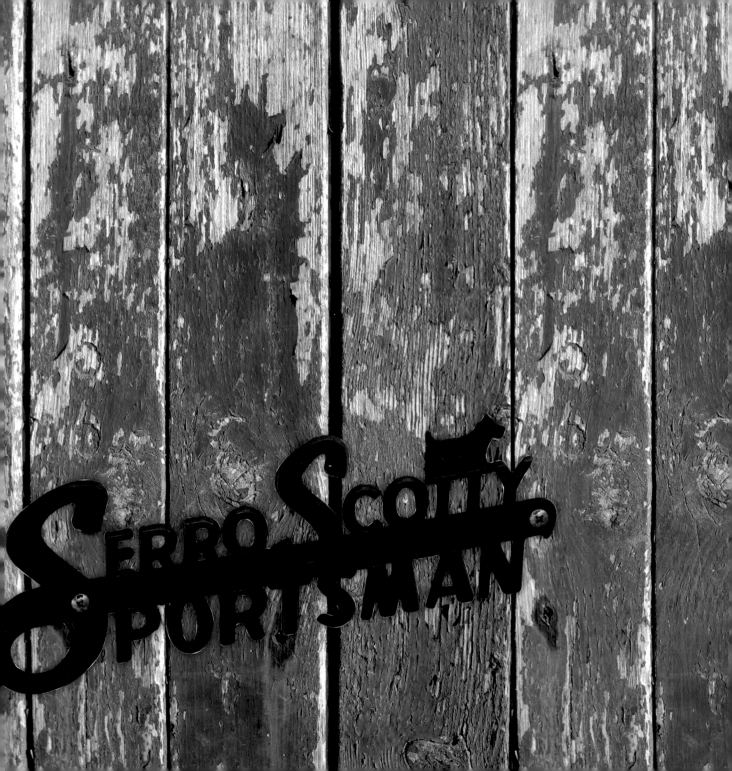

CONTENTS

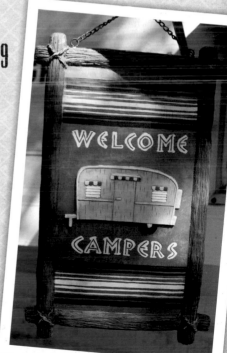

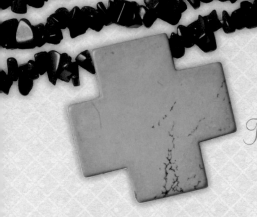

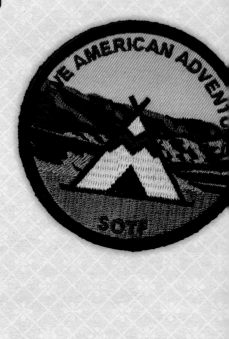

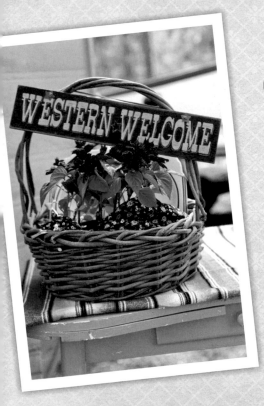

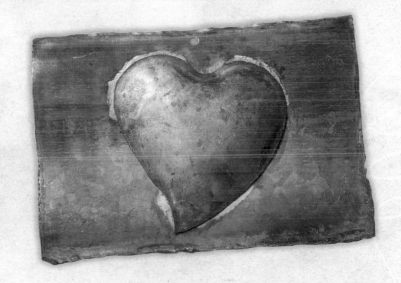

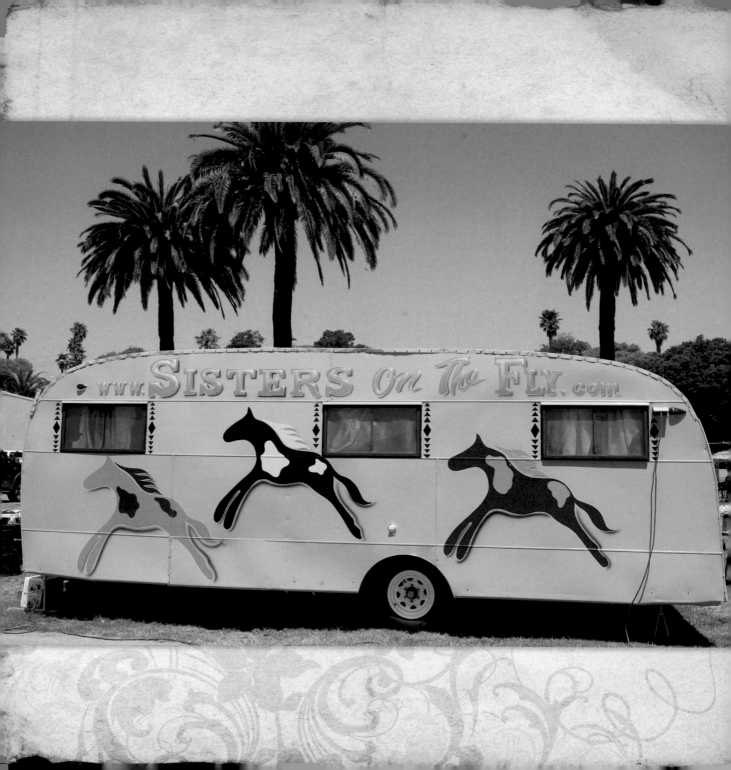

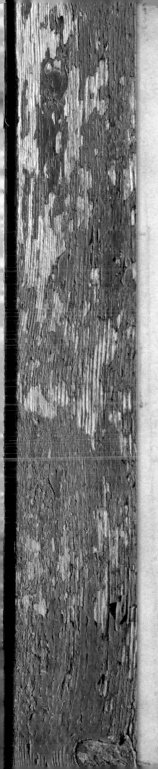

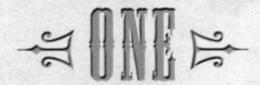

HOW IT ALL BEGAN

During the golden age of trailer travel, from the 1930s to the 1960s, Americans found it easier than ever to get away from it all while taking all the comforts of home with them. A new type of vacation was born that combined the adventure and economy of camping without the need to really "rough it."

In the next four decades, however, people began traveling almost exclusively by plane, overflying the national parks and roadside attractions that were a part of their childhood memories. At the same time, motor campers became more utilitarian but less interesting, as wood and aluminum gave way to molded plastic and vinyl.

Now, Sisters on the Fly—the little girls who climbed into the backs of the station wagons pulling their families' Airstream trailers on cross-country adventures—are rescuing these relics from fields, ranches, and farms. They are finding vintage trailers through want ads, in junkyards, and on the Internet. They are restoring their finds

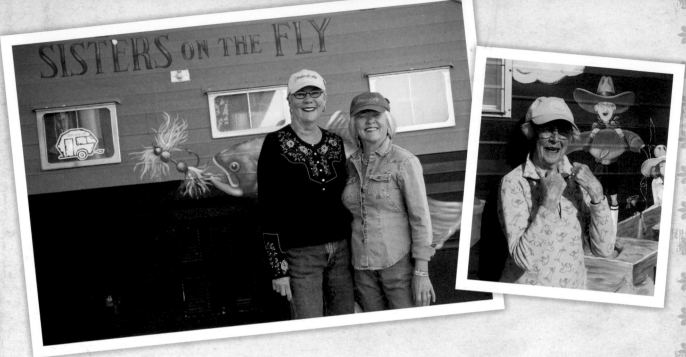

SISTERS ON THE FLY

to their original glory and creating comfortable spaces in which to make new travel memories.

"Our motto is 'We have more fun than anyone,'" says Maurrie Sussman (Sister #1), who, along with her real-life sister, Becky Clarke (Sister #2), are the founding Sisters. They were sitting in a drift boat in Montana one day, happily drinking a glass of wine in celebration of catching an eight-pound brown trout, and thought it would be so much fun to share the experience with friends. Maurrie won't say who actually caught that big trout, because "it is a fish tale, you know." She and Becky were taught how to fish by their mother, simply known as Mazie (Sister #4), when they were just little girls. Mazie also taught them the art of telling a good fish story.

The two sisters started Sisters on the Fly in 1999, a group that soon grew to a dozen members who met in Montana for fly-fishing. That dozen grew to more than 1,300 women all over the United States and Canada, each with a vintage trailer and a story about the trailer's history. The women range in age from twenty-eight to ninety. Many of their rigs are from the 1950s and 1960s, range from twelve to sixteen feet in length, and contain between 100 and 150 square feet of interior space. Models include the popular Shasta, Scotsman, Aloha, Airstream, Scotty, Holiday, Aljo, and Empire. "We find it so comfortable to drag our own bedrooms with us," says Maurrie. "After a hard day of fishing and having fun, it is pure bliss to fall into your own featherbed."

Indian ponies painted on the bed frame echo the trailer's exterior design. The buckskin curtains are hung up on arrows affixed to the wall by square nails.

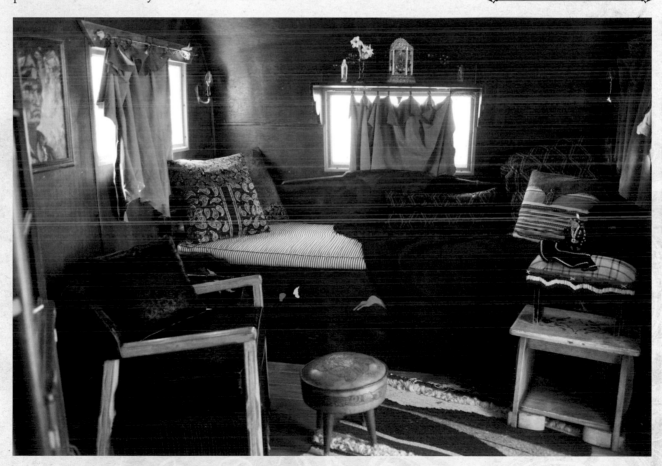

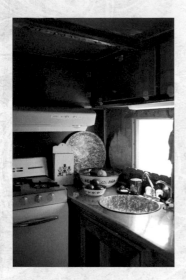

Becoming a Sister is not difficult. You don't have to fish, and you don't have to ride horses. You should have a trailer, but that, too, isn't always necessary as most of the Sisters are willing to share. (But you can be sure that before long you'll really want to have your own little portable playhouse!) So what does it take to become a Sister? Just one thing: You must want a Sister and want to be a Sister to some of the most independent, freedom-loving, warmhearted, and generous women in the world.

Sisters on the Fly meet in groups of ten or more on the Oregon coast, in the Smoky Mountains, on the great Midwestern plains, in the Ozarks, in the Shenandoah Valley, in Texas Hill Country, and on Tybee Island, Georgia. "We drive the two-lane back roads in a Cowgirl Caravan, and when we stop in the little towns everyone comes out to look at our trailers," Maurrie says. Sometimes they camp in a national park, sometimes in a rancher's meadow. "As long as it's near a beautiful stream, we're happy," she says.

But not all of the Sisters are into fishing. Some simply enjoy buying old trailers—sometimes two or three—fixing them up, caravanning to a beautiful spot, and camping out under the stars with "a great bunch of women who are not afraid to get out and do things," says Joyce Ufford (Sister #570).

They are indeed a diverse group—nurses, bookkeepers, kindergarten teachers, bakers, pet sitters, artists, school bus drivers, small business owners,

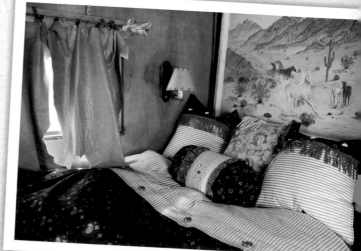

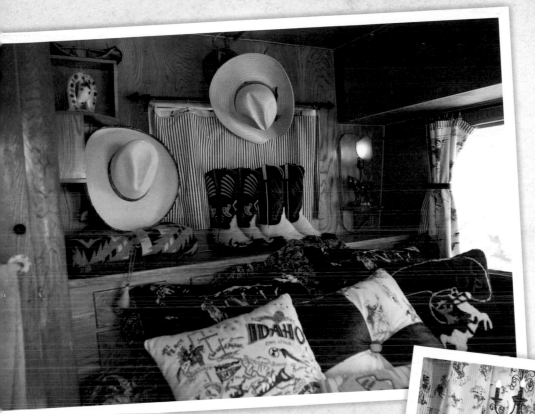

LEFT: Warm red pillows and some of Becky's well-worn (but still so cute) cowgirl boots decorate the bedroom area of Twisted Sister.

BELOW: Cowgirls love girly things—like bouquets of roses on the dinette table.

housewives, and mothers. "Self-sufficient women from every walk of life," is how Kris Woody (Sister #30), a retired airline attendant, describes the Sisters. "Sometimes they start out that way, but more often they become self-sufficient after being Sisters for a while."

What do they have in common? Most like to fish. All like to shop and have fun. They are great cooks and love to eat. They adore their husbands and children but are comfortable being on their own. They feel safe together. Most of all, they enjoy meeting new friends who, pretty soon, begin to feel like family.

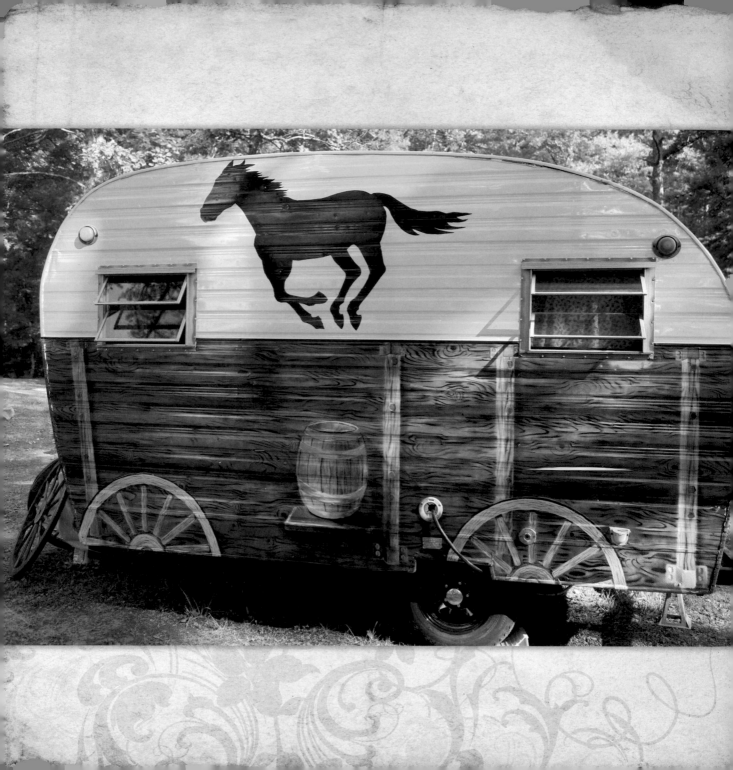

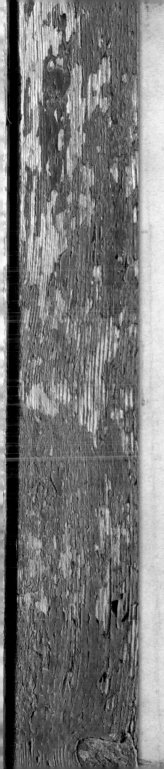

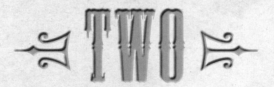

BUYING AND RESTORING A VINTAGE TRAILER

Maurrie Sussman (Sister #1) started collecting vintage trailers more than a decade ago. She has remodeled more than forty trailers for herself, for friends, and for women who have since become friends and Sisters. She still has her first trailer—a 1958 Holiday named Lucy—and remembers their first moments together. "She was trashed when I first saw her," says Maurrie, "but when I walked inside, I just fell in love."

Trailers from the 1950s and 1960s are in high demand because they are adorable and affordable. But, Maurrie cautions, you should make sure the frame is structurally sound before falling too deeply in love. When she buys a trailer, the first thing she does is scrub down every inch of the inside and outside—by hand. "With my hands, I get

PREVIOUS: Trompe l'oeil wagon wheels, logs, a whiskey barrel, and a trotting horse give a glimpse into the love Karen LeGlue (Sister #459) has for all things Western.

BELOW: Many of the Sisters seek out unloved vintage trailers that they can completely renovate to their exact specifications.

BELOW RIGHT: This Shasta awaits a Sister's TLC. There are many avenues for tracking down and acquiring old trailers. See chapter 13 for some of our favorite sources.

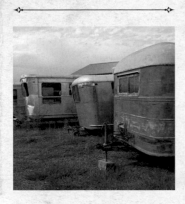

to know every square inch of my trailer," she says. "I also get a good feel for what's broken and what needs to be fixed or replaced."

The next thing is a fun step: choosing a name. Women's names such as Calamity Jane, Mustang Sally, Rhinestone Cowgirl, Whiskey Rose, Vaccarra Guerra, and Sister Sioux are favorites. Others include the Bunkhouse, Playin' Hookey, Hodge Podge Lodge, Lazy Ranch, Oasis, Hummingbird House, and, for one of the smallest, TexaLou's Roadhouse and Dance Hall. Some Sisters enjoy a play on words: Belle on Wheels, Porta Party, Reel Suite, and Roam Sweet Home are some good examples. According to Maurrie, once you choose a name, the decorating—both inside and out—just seems to fall into place.

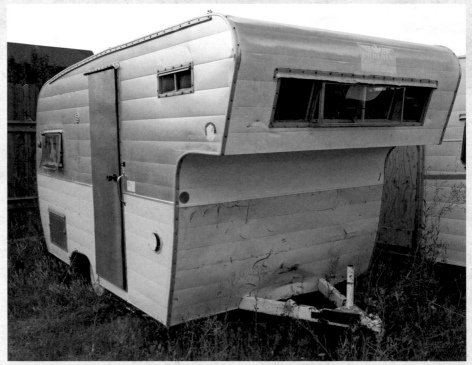

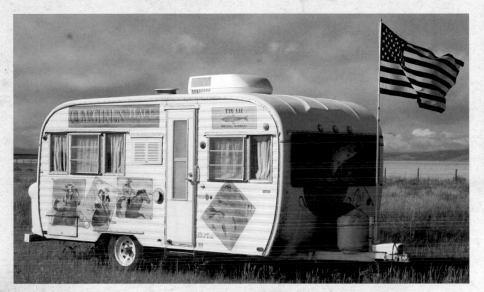

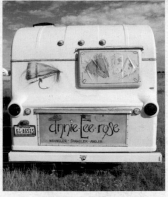

Sisters tell of finding their trailers just sitting in a farmer's field or a rancher's meadow. Sometimes they were allowed to just "haul that junk away." Other times they paid as little as fifty dollars. Sometimes trailers just "come to us," says Maurie, who tells about getting "the nicest note from a man whose grandfather passed away and left a 1959 Shasta sitting on his land. The man said he wanted to give the trailer to someone who could get as much enjoyment out of it as he had with his grandfather a long time ago."

A fully restored vintage trailer can cost more than $8,000, but most Sisters agree they'd rather do the work themselves (an appealingly old-fashioned idea in these cash-strapped times). They rely on one another for expertise, encouragement, and simple here's-how-I-did-that advice. It can take a year or more to restore a trailer if you're doing all the work yourself, but each Sister recalls the bone-deep satisfaction of hooking up her self-created masterpiece and driving to a Sisters event.

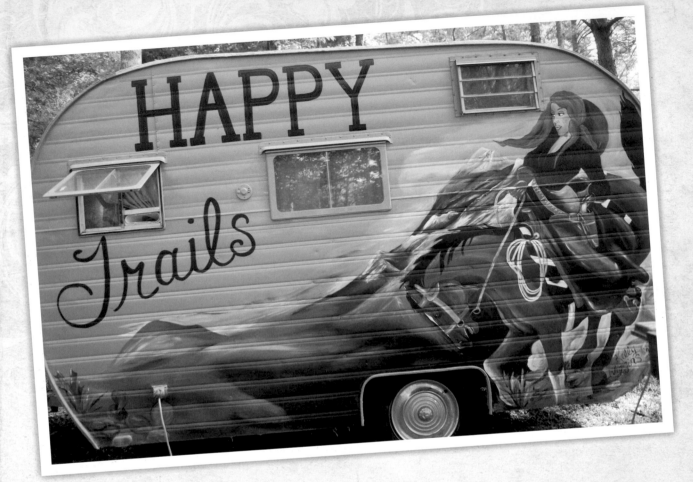

ABOVE: Named Happy Trails, this 1958 Winnebago sports a Western-themed mural and belongs to Linda Brede (Sister #250). The artwork is by Kelly Wiggins; it is the first trailer she ever painted.

OPPOSITE: Becky Clarke stands outside Twisted Sister, a trailer she restored from top to bottom. It took six months to sand and finish the outside.

Debra Bolnik (Sister #45) can laugh now when she remembers the travails of restoring her first trailer, a 1962 Kencraft, but at the time, it was "a humbling experience." The restoration took six months, and she did it all by hand. One morning, hearing on the radio that a big winter storm was coming in, she threw a warm coat over her flannel pajamas and hurried outside to put a final coat of sealant on the trailer's roof.

A construction crew was working on the house next door. In a situation that could have been written for an episode of *I Love Lucy*, Debra suddenly realized that the seat of her pajama bottoms was stuck to the roof of her trailer. "I had two choices," she recalls. "I could either drop my drawers in front of the construction crew and climb off that trailer or wait until my husband woke up. I'll leave it up to you to guess what I did." The trailer, which she calls Annie Lee Rose, is named for her husband and two daughters.

In time, she bought and restored trailers for each of her daughters and turned her love of vintage trailers into a restoration business called Montana Camps and Cabins. "I just started collecting and couldn't stop," she says. When she had more than a dozen "waifs and strays" parked all around her house, "it was time to open up a shop." She compares her trailers to racehorses: "Beautiful at one time, then put out to pasture. I'm bringing them back again, one by one." Because Debra has restored more than thirty trailers, she, along with Maurrie and Becky Clarke (Sister #2), are knowledgeable resources the Sisters regularly turn to when they are working on their own trailers.

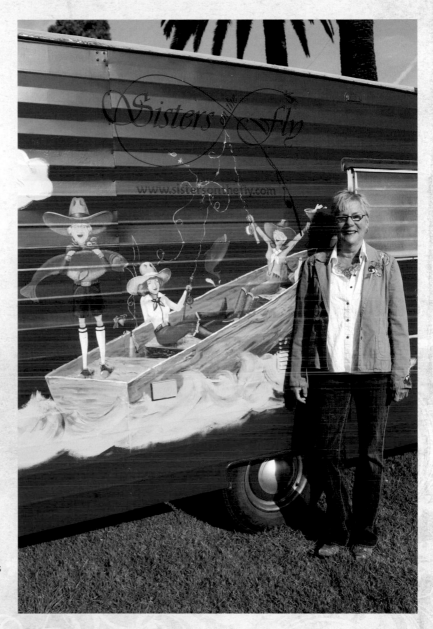

FROM START TO FINISH WITH DEBRA BOLNIK

Debra Bolnik says that she's seen it all. "I learned the hard way not to fall in love [with a trailer] too hard or too fast," she says. One of her first trailers was rotted so badly that she had to tear out and replace the entire front end. She found a dead rattlesnake (and a lot of mouse skins) between the interior and exterior walls of another of her trailers. In yet another, she discovered huge holes through which you could see the highway (they had been covered up with brand-new linoleum).

Denise Saldana-Beste (Sister #761) stands in front of her 1958 Chinook, Shantilly Lace. When she bought it, her brother-in-law called it a shanty and the name stuck.

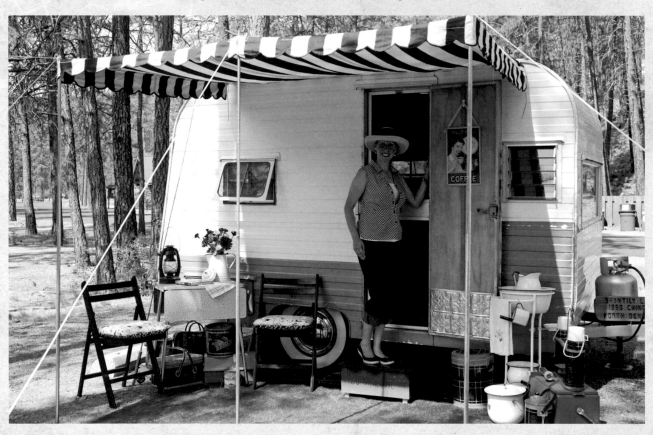

Her rules are simple and few; if you follow them, you'll save yourself money and heartache.

Before she buys, she takes the trailer to an RV center to have all the mechanics checked out. These old trailers have been sitting outside for years—or even decades—parked behind barns, left in windbreaks, or used as storage sheds or as shelters for animals. The axles need to be greased and the bearings greased and packed. The electrical and propane lines must be checked, because even a pin hole in a propane line can cause an explosion and fire.

The next expense: brand-new trailer tires and a braking system. "Your trailer is lighter than your car and can go faster, especially on the downhill stretches; a new braking system means your trailer will not be coming up over your bumper," she explains.

Make sure you get a clear title. Then, start thinking about what you're going to spend a lot of money on: flooring (don't touch it if you don't have to, because it probably contains asbestos); kitchen counters (a lot of the old ones have cigarette burns); and an air conditioner (where will you put it, and can your trailer generate enough energy to run it?).

When she finally gets the trailer to her shop, Debra washes the outside with vinegar and water and then sands it. She recommends taking it to a business that specializes in painting automobiles, because house paint will start flaking in just a few years. Painting the exterior will cost between $800 and $1,500 for a small trailer, which is money well spent, says Debra. "It lasts forever, and the paint shop will fill whatever small pits and dings you may have missed."

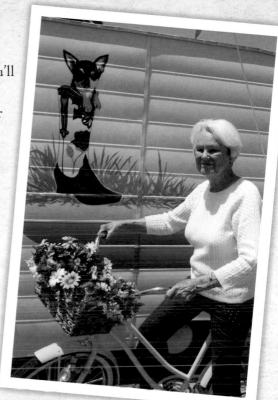

Li'l Loafer, a 1964 Aristocrat belonging to Zola Liner (Sister #682), is painted a pale green (with a bike to match) and features her beloved doggie sitting in a cowgirl boot.

FROM START TO FINISH WITH BECKY CLARKE

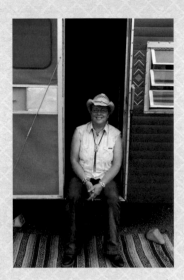

ABOVE: Carol Hill (Sister #335) owns three trailers, and each has a different name and mood. This one, Sipapu Lodge, has a soulful, Native American feel.

OPPOSITE: After Carol Hill tore her 1962 Go Tag Along down to the frame, she decided to do something unconventional: She added a fireplace and a big easy chair.

Becky had to strap on snowshoes to get the first look at her trailer. "It was filled with dirty dishes and dirty clothes," she says. Later, snowshoeing back to her car, she was thinking that it was the most disgusting trailer she'd ever seen. Spring came and the trailer was still available. Now it was sitting in a mountain meadow full of wildflowers. Becky looked inside and, able to see past the dirt and grime and the mouse-chewed dinette cushions, discovered the trailer's potential. She pulled the trailer to her back pasture and got to work.

During the cleaning and restoration, she found maps from the 1950s and 1960s—the last time this trailer had been on the road. "I put my mask on and started sanding," she says. It took six months to sand and finish the outside. Because she prefers doing the work herself, she painted the exterior with Rust-Oleum paint, using a roller. Right then, the other Sisters gave the trailer her name: Twisted Sister. The exterior mural of three women fishing was painted by Vickie Stoppello's (Sister #5) daughter, Rachel, a children's book illustrator.

Inside, Becky attacked the moldy fridge and crusty stove. "The appliances are of the period and made to fit the specific spaces in the trailer," she says, and worth the effort to save. After lots of sweat and sore muscles, the stove, oven, and minifridge all work. The vintage fridge even makes cute little ice cubes, shaped like—what else?—cowgirl boots.

MORE TRAILER STORIES

"At first my husband didn't quite get it," says Denise Saldana-Beste (Sister #761), "but I took him to a rally that included vintage cars pulling vintage trailers, and then he totally got it." Now Denise has two trailers,

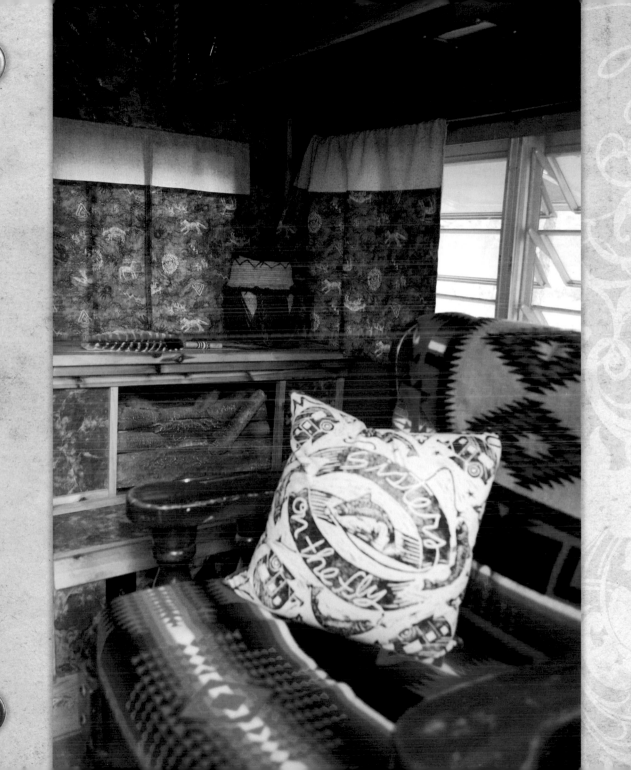

a 1961 Aljo and a 1958 Chinook, which take up most of the garage. Her husband helps fix them up and says that their cars are replaceable, but the trailers are not. Denise's trailer, Shantilly Lace, was accidentally named by a brother-in-law who, seeing the trailer in its shabby, still unrestored state, blurted out, "Whose shanty is that?"

Jan Dylewski (Sister #550) is only the second owner of her 1958 Shasta Airflyte. The previous owner had bought it new and took it camping with kids and grandkids for more than fifty years. "He advertised [in the classifieds on http://www.tincantourists.com] that he wanted someone who would love it and take care of it like he had." Her father laughed when, after she bought her trailer, she asked for power tools for Christmas. Now, he happily gives her tools—not only for Christmas, but for each birthday as well.

Carol Hill (Sister #335) is a middle school counselor and has three trailers. One is decorated like a beach, another in a cowgirl theme, and a third, Sipapu Lodge, in a more soulful Native American motif with a twist. When she bought this 1966 Go-Tag-Along, it was in such bad shape that she had to take it down to the metal. Suddenly, she was struck with the thought of putting in a fireplace. Her trailer doesn't have any of the traditional trappings, but it does have a big easy chair and a beautiful gas fireplace—perfect for relaxing after a long day out on the water.

IMPORTANT DOS AND DON'TS

Dos

1. Before you buy, take your trailer to an RV place and have everything—axles, bearings, and propane lines—thoroughly checked.

2. Get a clear title. Otherwise, you won't be able to get insurance or a license, and you can't take your trailer on the road without those.
3. Pay with cash if you can; you'll often get a better deal.
4. Put on brand-new trailer tires.
5. Check the tire rims. If they are the old-fashioned split rims, change them to single rims; split rims have been known to cause blowouts.

Don'ts

1. Never buy a trailer sight unseen!
2. Don't buy a trailer that's been used for ice fishing. It usually has a hole cut in the floor, which weakens the trailer's structural integrity.
3. Don't paint the exterior with ordinary house paint, because it will start wearing off in a few years. Use automotive paint.
4. Don't buy a trailer with water damage unless you can locate the source of the leak.
5. Don't buy a trailer that's been attacked by termites.

While this last caveat may seem just a tad humorous, termites can be the death of your trailer. Debra Bolnik recalls traveling behind Cathlene Fishman (Sister #35) when the windows of Cathlene's cute new vintage trailer began flying off one by one on the way to a Sisters event. Each time it happened, the Sisters stopped and, using duct tape, remounted the windows. During one of these stops, they discovered termites "living in every inch" of the wood structure of the trailer. The wood was so infested that the trailer was no longer roadworthy. Fearing for the safety of their own trailers, "we made Cathlene park her trailer yards and yards away from the other trailers," says Debra.

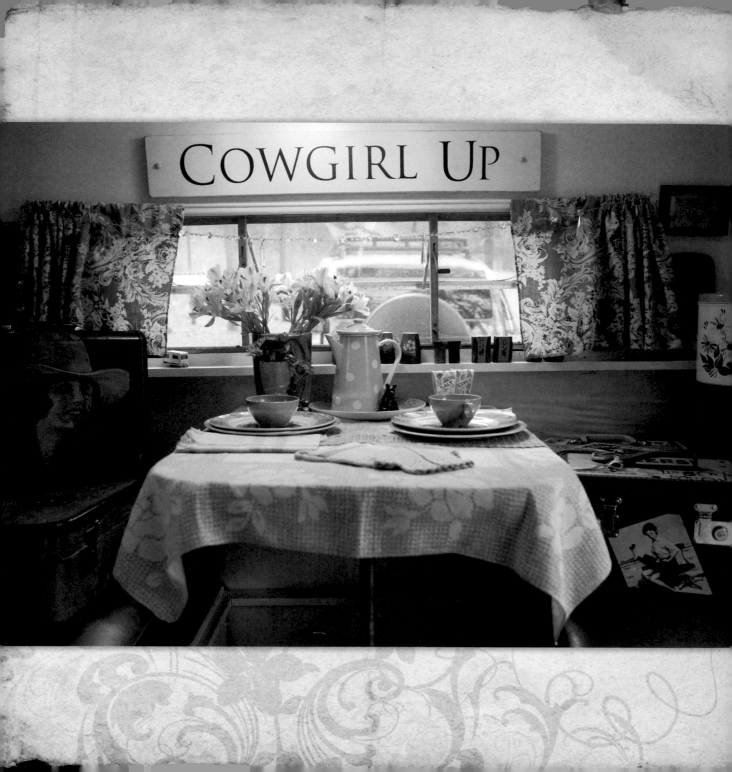

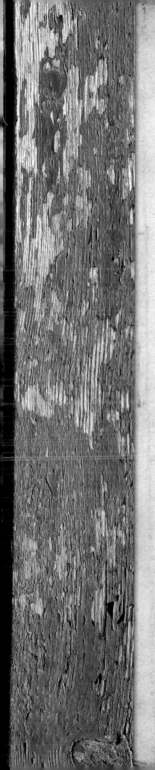

THREE

TRAILER DECOR, INSIDE AND OUT

Now that the hard work is behind you, the real fun begins. Your trailer's decor reflects your personality—or more precisely, your personality as a Sister. We all know that underneath a Sister's coveralls and mud-caked cowgirl boots, there are bare legs, a skirt, and pretty lingerie.

A Sister plays many roles, and she can morph from a farmhand to a substitute teacher in a flash; from being a full-time mom to dancing the two-step at Cowgirl Prom. With a little lipstick and a fluffing of the hair, a Sister makes a lovely dinner companion, even after wielding a fence stretcher and hammer to fix the fence on the way to that fancy restaurant in town.

The names Sisters give to their trailers—humorous, silly, serious,

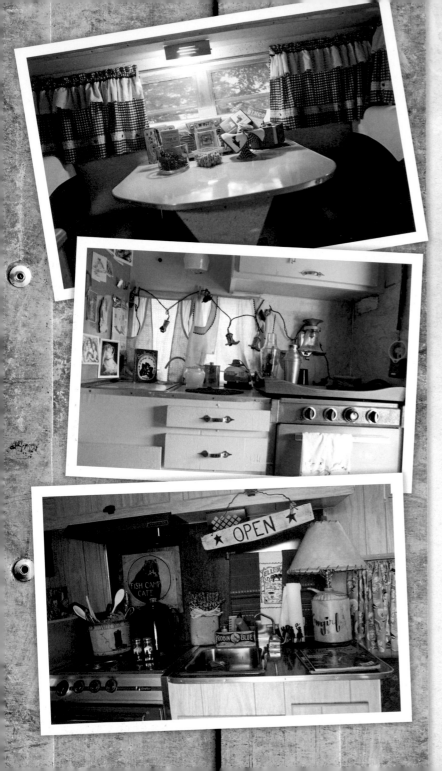

or historical—not only reflect their own personalities but also influence the decor. For example, Miss Floozy, the trailer belonging to Vicky "Don't like that cowgirl stuff" Kimling (Sister #94), is decorated in fishnet, black lace, and pink marabou feather boas. Peggy Burns (Sister #229), a school librarian, named her trailer Peggy Sue after herself and decorated it—inside and out—with huge pop-art daisies in eye-popping colors. L'il Loafer, the trailer belonging to Zola Liner (Sister #682), is completely decorated in serene Martha Stewart green, with a shiny green bike to match.

Debra Bolnik (Sister #45) had an antiques store and, being a Texas cowgirl, enjoys decorating all of her trailers in a Western motif. Her mirrors are made out of old horseshoes, and she hangs her hats on a rack made of cow horns near vintage signs that read "Dancing Tonight" and "God Bless Cowgirls." She tries to make sure everything in her trailer is both practical and fun. She uses wire baskets, hanging from buffalo nickel–fronted knobs, for storage. The antique cutting board that covers up her Formica counter can be used as a drinks tray, a nightstand, or a card table (the Sisters love to play poker for pennies).

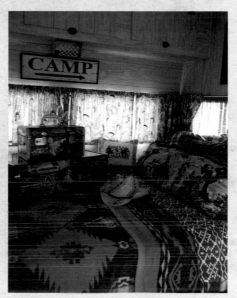

Everything in her trailer is screwed down or bolted to the wall, including her spice rack, so that after traveling along a bumpy road for several hours she can open her trailer and find everything just where she put it at the beginning of the journey.

One thing Debra never does is paint the interior of her trailer. Nor will she buy a trailer in which the wood (usually birch) has been painted. She notes that sometimes the vintage trailer interiors are painted to cover up water damage, and interior paint can devalue a vintage trailer by as much as $1,000. "It is best to keep things as original as possible," she says. She does, however, paint the interiors of her kitchen cabinets with a special bug-retardant paint because "I want my trailer to be as clean as my house."

Becky Clarke (Sister #2) is an interior designer who has decorated luxurious homes and log lodges throughout the West, but her favorite projects are the trailers (she's restored and decorated four for herself and dozens for other Sisters). Because she loves earth tones, she uses a lot of browns, reds, and dark greens "for warmth and cheer . . . and because they don't really show dirt." She replaced her chipped Formica kitchen

PREVIOUS: Pink dishes and floral fabrics add a "girly" touch to the rugged cowgirl theme. Vintage cloth tablecloths and linen napkins are easy to find and are necessary luxuries for feeling at home on the road.

OPPOSITE TOP: Inspired by a 1950s diner, this delightful booth features sleek red leather seats and handmade checkered café curtains.

OPPOSITE MIDDLE: Green cabinets brighten up the small space, while a collection of notes and postcards remind a traveling Sister of faraway friends.

OPPOSITE BOTTOM: Complementing the orange stove, a collection of blue and orange items makes this kitchen both functional and stylish.

LEFT: Layers of quilts topped with a vintage camp blanket makes for a comfy place to snuggle into after a day of outdoor activities. Decoupaged train cases provide pretty storage for toiletries.

counters with tin because it is durable, period-appropriate, and much less expensive than copper or pounded copper.

For some extra bling in the tiny dining room, she hung a little crystal chandelier, and she placed small mirrors made out of vintage tin ceiling tiles throughout her trailer to make the twelve-foot-long space seem larger. Silver-framed family photos reflect the twinkly lights tucked into her bookcases and strung along the window frames. She says Sisters can save money by doing a lot of the work, such as sewing curtains and cushions, themselves but suggests that great bedding is a good investment: She recommends "a feather mattress and a down comforter . . . so when we're traveling, we can have the best hotel room in the world."

How do you know when you're finished decorating? "My sister, Maurrie, and I have a pretty simple rule," says Becky. "Hook your trailer up and take it for a ride. Everything that ends up on the floor is too much."

At least one of the Sisters, Pam Heron (Sister #79), also known as the Queen of Pamalot, does not subscribe to the less-is-more theory of trailer decor. "More is always better," she says, standing inside her 1965 Shasta,

BELOW: A pink chenille bedspread and lace curtains are delightfully feminine. Wall hangings tell the story of this Sister's travels.

BELOW RIGHT: Pam Heron (Sister #79), aka the "Queen of Pamalot," was a homemaker for forty years. "Now it's my turn," she says, posing outside her trailer, which is parked beside a rushing stream.

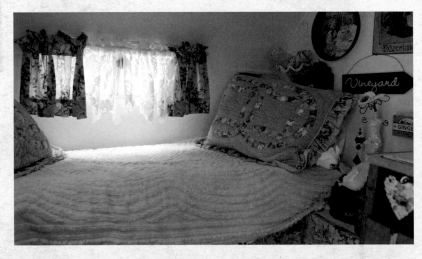

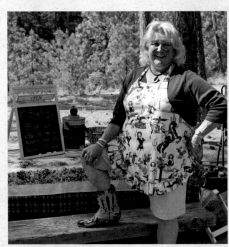

in which every square inch is covered with pillows, vintage linens, decoupaged train cases, and, displayed prominently in the tiny kitchen, a heavy silver cowgirl boot that serves as a wine cooler. "I was a homemaker raising kids for forty years; now it is my turn," she says. Indeed, her bed is piled high with pillows that proclaim her royalty—in embroidery and rhinestones.

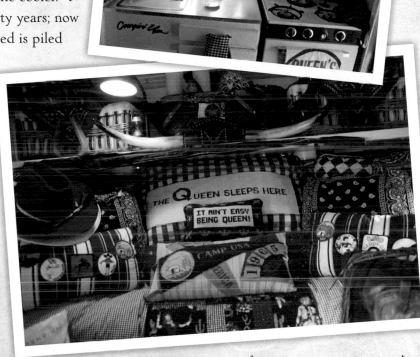

Swanee Owen (Sister #864) bought her trailer, a 1962 Little Gem, on Craigslist two years ago. "I paid $3,800 for it, which is quite a lot, but I got just what I wanted," she says, "and the owner showed me exactly what he had done to restore it." Her trailer is decorated in a red and white pop tech style because she "hates clutter," and is called The Ant Bed Lodge. "I'm plagued by ants every time I go camping; that's why I chose an ant influenced decor."

Vintage funeral home fans and sassy aprons from the 1950s are the cornerstones of the decor of Southern Sister Paula Bush (Sister #870). Her trailer, Honky Tonk Angel, is full of collectibles, but every single one of them is put to good use. Sisters often ask to borrow some of her fans to keep cool during the day and, at dusk, to keep the air moving to discourage hungry mosquitoes.

TOP: The tiny kitchen is filled with Pam's personality and style without feeling oppressive or cluttered. Careful editing is the key: Keep only what you love, and it will look perfect.

BOTTOM: An obvious affinity for the color red sets the stage for Pam's delightfully over the top sleeping space, fit for a queen.

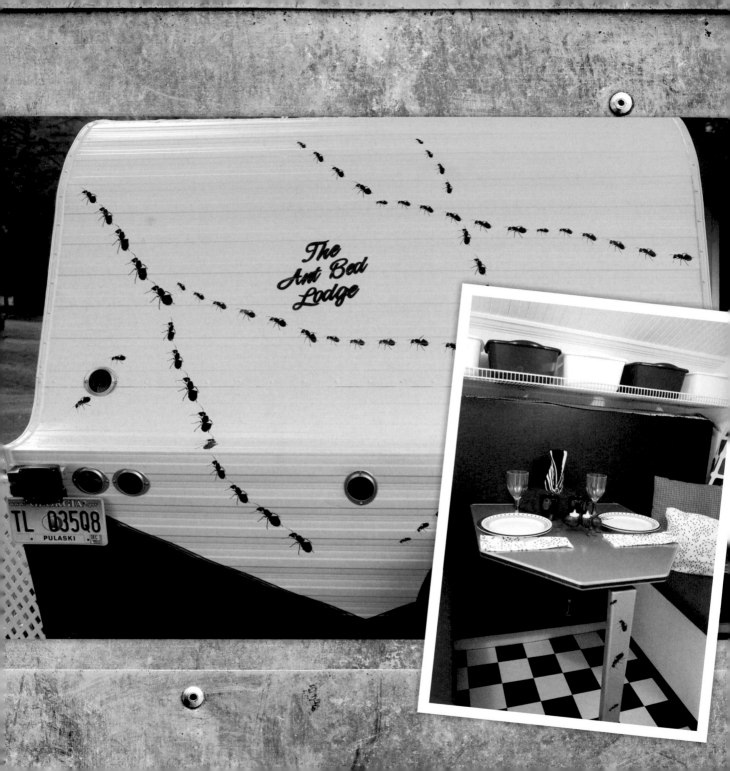

Tips for Living Large in a Small Space

1. Take advantage of your built-ins. Store your linens under the dinette seats. Bookcases—especially those with restraining rails to hold in the books—can also be used for tin dishes or plastic martini glasses.

2. Create storage for your clothing out of vintage suitcases, and use old train cases (Grace Kelly chic!) for your makeup and toiletries.

3. No space should be unused or underused. Every space should have a dual use.

4. Create an outdoor living area—with a table, chairs, a comfortable chaise, and some colorful plants, such as pots of geraniums or herbs, like lavender.

5. Layer your lighting with lamps, strings of holiday lights, small lights tucked into bookshelves, and the soft glow of near-ceiling lights.

6. Use mirrors to visually expand your space, to reflect light, and, of course, to take a final look at your fine self before you walk out of your trailer.

7. Think vertically. Use stripes or tall lines to lead the eye upward.

8. Save precious counter space by getting furniture and appliances to scale. Even flat-screen TVs come in small sizes and can be mounted to the wall.

9. Have fun playing with fabrics, colors, and patterns, but stay within the same color palette.

10. This one is the most important: Ignore the previous suggestions. Do whatever you like and have fun!

OPPOSITE: Every time Swanee Owen (Sister #864) goes camping, ants are sure to follow, so she named her trailer The Ant Bed Lodge and uses ants as her theme. As founding Sister Maurrie Sussman explains, once you name your trailer, the decorating just seems to fall into place.

INSET: The bold red, white, and black theme continues inside with fun fabrics, whimsical accessories, and, of course, the ants.

BELOW: A white background keeps things visually clean, while retro-inspired fabric offers a contemporary touch. Having a constant theme (in this case, ants) makes for focused shopping excursions and flea market hunts.

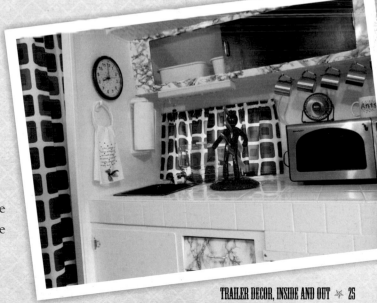

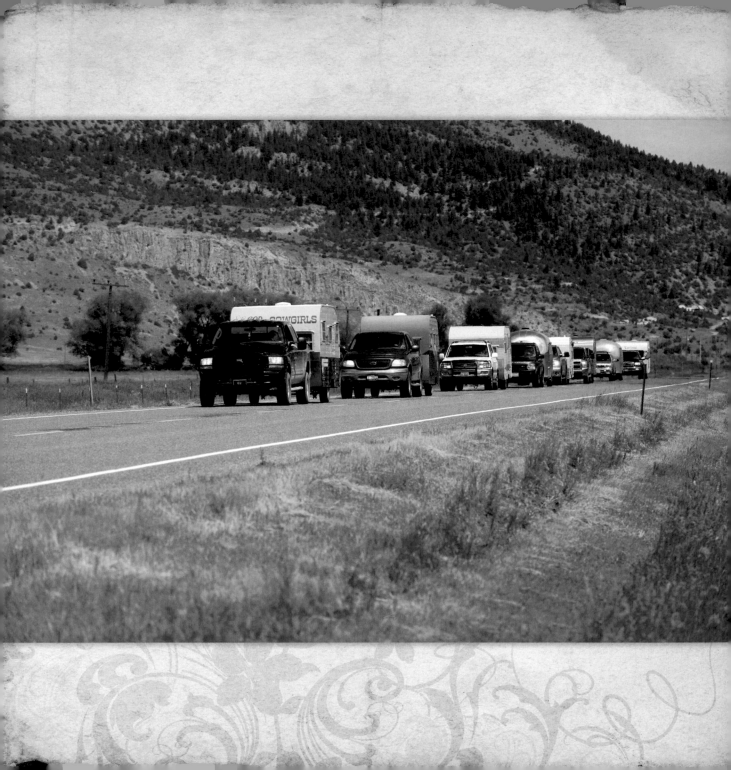

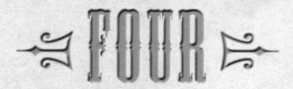

FOUR

ON THE ROAD

Buying a vintage trailer is a thrill, but in case you skipped chapter 2, make sure it is roadworthy before taking your trailer on the road—starting with the tires, axles, bearings, and propane lines. Maurrie Sussman (Sister #1) always buys brand-new trailer tires before taking a new trailer for a drive. "The first thing a girl needs is new shoes," she says. Then she makes sure the electrical system works so she can hook up her lights. "Every girl likes a little bling," Maurrie adds, laughing. It's not very expensive to replace an axle or repack bearings, but Maurrie is leery about buying a trailer that has been flipped—that is, blown down or blown over in the wind. Chances are the frame is bent and the trailer will never pull well again.

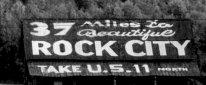

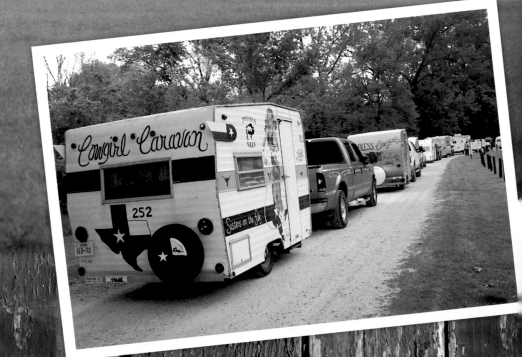

DOES IT PULL WELL?

"Pulling well" is so important that it's often the first question a Sister asks when she's buying a trailer: "Does it pull well?" If your trailer pulls well, you will hardly feel it behind your car or truck. It "sits lightly" on your trailer hitch. It is aerodynamically designed and well balanced. It performs well in windy conditions and in the snow. On the other hand, if your trailer doesn't pull well, it will be a huge drag on your car's engine. It will lean too far into and out of curves. If it leans out far enough in windy or snowy weather, it can blow over—taking your truck with it. Although no Sister has ever had a blow over, some have come close.

A group of Sisters were driving in the desert once, on their way home from a fishing trip, when a huge windstorm came up and one of the Sisters' trailers began leaning much too far. The Sisters put her in the middle of the caravan, thinking this would break the wind. It worked. They limped along to the next town, found a mechanic who diagnosed and solved the problem (a broken leaf spring—part of the U-joint that holds the axle to the bottom of the trailer). A trip that should have taken three hours took more than twenty, but true to their motto: "Sisters don't leave Sisters behind."

Maurrie also says to stay away from any trailer that has been rain damaged "unless you want to take it down to zero and rebuild the entire trailer." Some Sisters fall in love with water-damaged trailers and buy and restore them, but leaks in the trailer's

PREVIOUS: A caravan sticks together as the Sisters head toward their next adventure. It's great fun to travel in groups, but it's also much safer—these gals watch out for one another. "We never leave anyone behind," says Maurrie.

OPPOSITE: The journey is half the fun. The Sisters always take the back roads to their destinations and enjoy some of the most stunning landscapes in the country. (They also look for fun, out-of-the-way shops and markets.)

INSET: Sisters from all over the country gather in groups of ten or more trailers—sometimes there are as many as sixty—to ride horses, fish, and reconnect with their Sisters. *Photo courtesy Christi Partee (Sister #687)*

BELOW: The Cowgirl Caravan circles down to a camping spot near the perfect fishing stream.

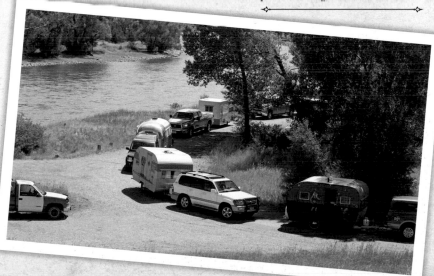

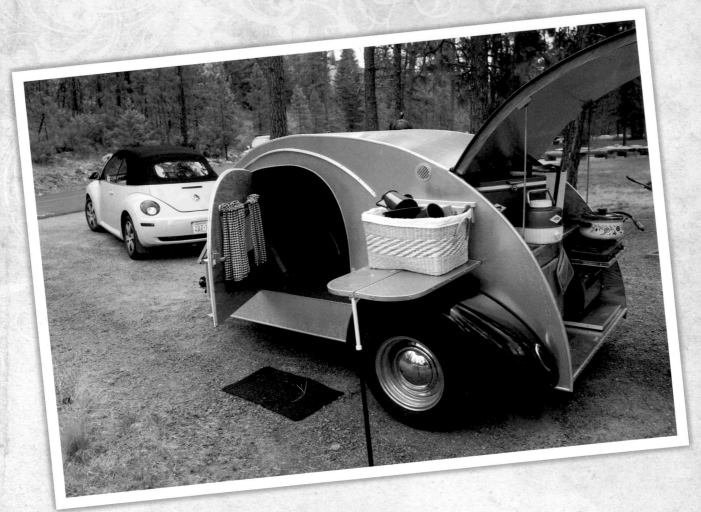

A simple teardrop trailer pulled by a convertible VW Bug New Beetle is all this Sister needs to enjoy the romance of the open road.

skin must be found and fixed. A trailer has to be sealed tight or you can spend a lot of money decorating the inside only to have it ruined in the first big rainstorm. Sometimes the solution can be as simple as putting new weather stripping on the door and windows. Sometimes, finding the leak can prove to be nearly impossible. If you love your trailer enough, you'll learn to live with small water stains—many of the Sisters do.

HOW MUCH POWER DO YOU NEED?

How big a rig does it take to pull a trailer? A little trailer, such as a Teardrop, Tab, or Casita, is light enough to be pulled by something as small as a Volkswagen New Beetle or GTI. A larger trailer, such as a Shasta, Holiday, or Play-Mor, needs a half-ton SUV or truck with a minimum of 200 horsepower. "But we like to have 350, especially if we'll be climbing mountains," says Maurrie. Vintage cars from the 1940s and 1950s are nearly always heavy enough and have six- or eight-cylinder engines that are well designed for towing.

LEARNING TO DRIVE WITH A TRAILER IN TOW

Driving a car or truck with a trailer is not as difficult as you may think, but it does take a little time and practice to learn how. Once you learn, though, it is a bit like riding a bicycle: You never forget how to do it. Becky Clarke (Sister #2) drives her trailer with ease. Because she's a patient teacher, she's the one most often called to teach new Sisters how to drive and, more important, how to back up. Her method is simple. "I'm going to come over," she says. "We're going to hook up your trailer and you're going to drive it. I'm going to ride with you and tell you what to do."

A big-box store parking lot (when the store is closed) is a good place to learn. First you

For the larger trailers, a minimum 200 horsepower half-ton truck or SUV works best, but cars from the 1940s and 1950s are usually heavy enough to do the job.

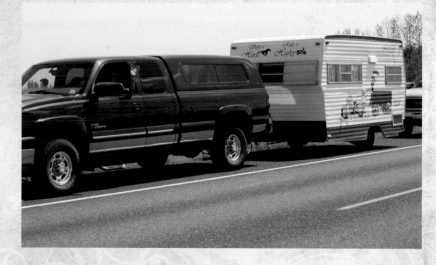

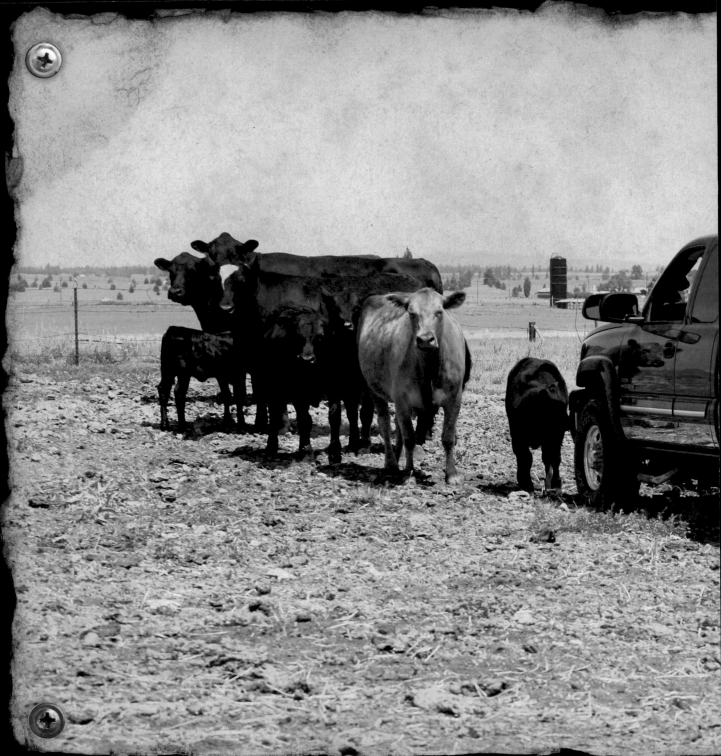

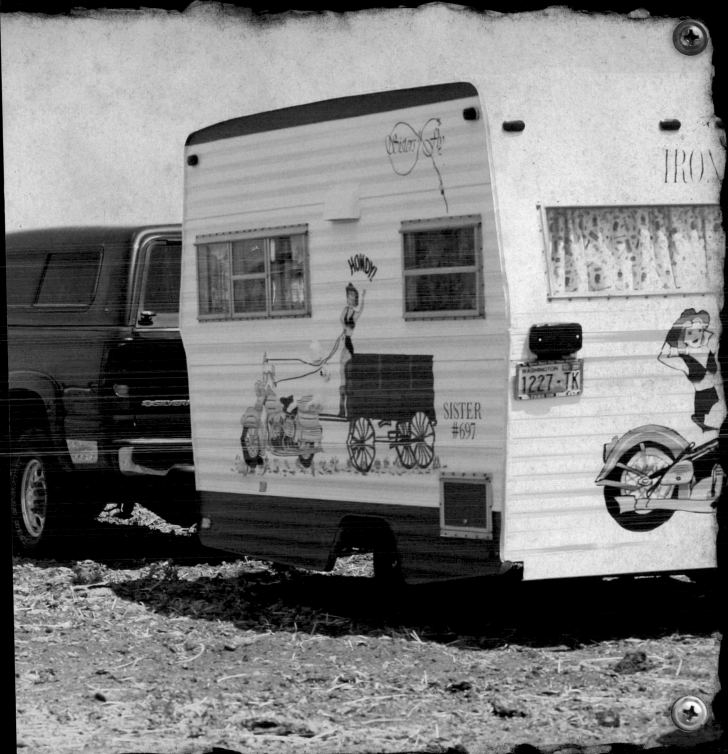

learn how to drive forward. You feel how your car or truck reacts to the added weight, and you get comfortable with that. Then, you drive in ever-widening circles.

"Backing up is a trick," Becky says, adding that a single axle is more difficult to back up than a double axle. The secret is to practice, practice, practice: Back up enough to learn how a trailer feels when it is being backed up properly and not jackknifing.

But even with all that help and encouragement, some Sisters don't ever learn how to back up. They just hook up their trailers and drive forward, knowing that when they arrive another Sister will help them back up into a camping spot. Maurrie still remembers a call from a first-time Sister who wanted to come to an event but was worried about driving—particularly about backing up. Maurrie told her: "Drive like you're driving your car and, when you park, leave yourself plenty of room to pull forward. Don't get stuck. Just get here and we'll take care of you."

ROAD WARRIORS: STORIES FROM THE ROAD

Although everything usually goes smoothly, there are always disasters—large and small—that seem horrible while they are happening but make good campfire stories later. Marty Knight (Sister #669) tells about a breakdown while she was heading to join a Sisters caravan with her elderly mother, who was in a wheelchair and on oxygen. They sat by the side of the road until a woman picked them up and took them to the nearest town (Vale, Oregon—thirty-five miles away) to find a mechanic. "I am so grateful to her and still send Christmas cards to that very, very nice lady," says Marty.

Debra Bolnik (Sister #45) describes a time when she was driving another Sister's car and trailer. When she got up to 45 mph, the trailer

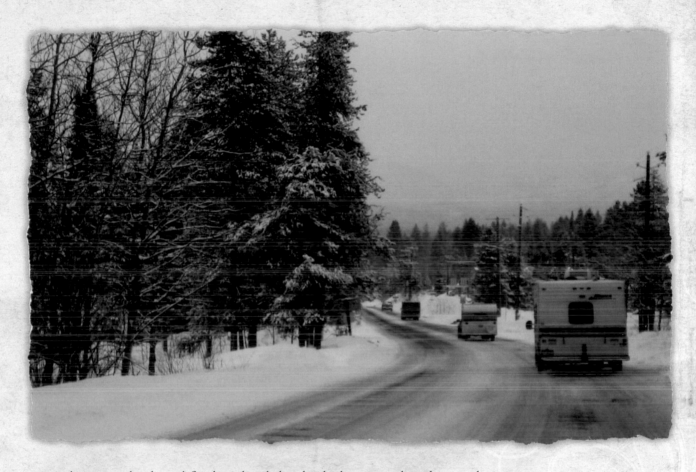

started swaying back and forth so hard that both the car and trailer nearly turned over. Everyone in the cars behind her started crying, thinking Debra was a goner. Luckily she was able to stop the car. The next stop was El Paso—for new tires, new sway bars, a new bumper (the old one had gotten too badly twisted), and a new towing package.

The buddy system (you get yourself a buddy and watch out for each other) works well most of the time, but everyone talks about the time Vickie Stoppello (Sister #5) was left behind in Missoula, Montana. All the Sisters had gone into a food market to stock up before a big visit to Glacier National Park. Vicki got stuck in the bathroom and, when she came out, the Sisters caravan was gone. After an hour on the road (and well out of cell phone range), someone noticed that Vickie's Rhinestone Cowgirl was missing. The caravan turned around and headed back.

Another memorable "war story" comes from Cathlene Fishman (Sister #35). Driving on an overpass looking down on the Pacific Ocean on Highway 101 in California, Cathlene lost her trailer. It came off her hitch and started rolling slowly backward down the highway. Just in time, the other Sisters in the caravan stopped the trailer, pulled it back onto the hitch, and made sure the lock on the hitch was engaged and working properly.

There are always flat tires, and there are always Sisters who know how to fix them. There was not one but two flats when more than fifty Sisters were caravanning to the National Cowgirl Museum and Hall of Fame in Fort Worth, Texas. On a major highway—Interstate 35—with cars and trucks whizzing by, the tires were quickly changed and the Sisters were back on the road.

COWGIRL CARAVAN

Sisters on the Fly travel in caravans for several reasons. It is fun to travel with lots of other Sisters, communicating and chatting by walkie-talkie along the way. It is safer to travel in a group. In case something goes wrong with one of the trailers, there's always a Sister who can diagnose the problem and has the right tools to fix it—at least for a while.

Tani Gibson (Sister #120), known to her Sisters as "T," is a dairy farmer from Junction City, Oregon. She's practical, a little gruff, and certainly a no-nonsense woman who milks more than five hundred cows a day. It is no surprise that her trailer is called Moo Fly and decorated in a black and white cow pattern—inside and out. She's a crackerjack fly fisher and, when on the road with the Sisters, she can fix nearly any mechanical problem that comes up. And she's always happy to help those Sisters who can drive forward but can't back up their trailers into a camping spot.

But the most important reason that the Sisters travel in Cowgirl Caravans is the attention they generate. In every little town and at every junction in between, "astonished passengers of passing cars smile and give us thumbs up as we roll along. When we stop, women are captivated by our adventure and take pictures of us and our trailers—celebrities for another day," says Kathy Wolfe who, along with her partner, Barbara Verhage, shares the honor of being Sister #10.

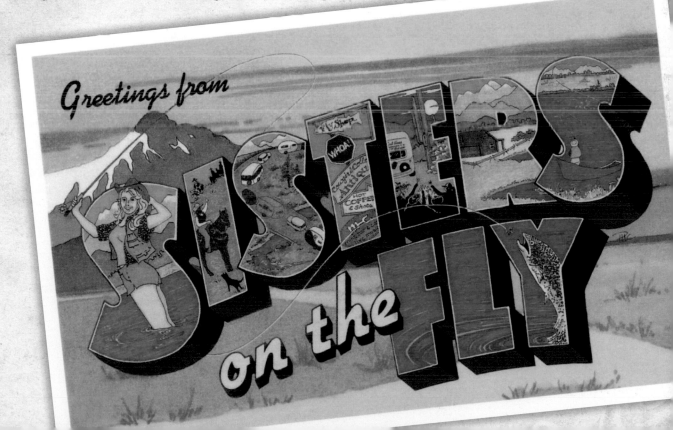

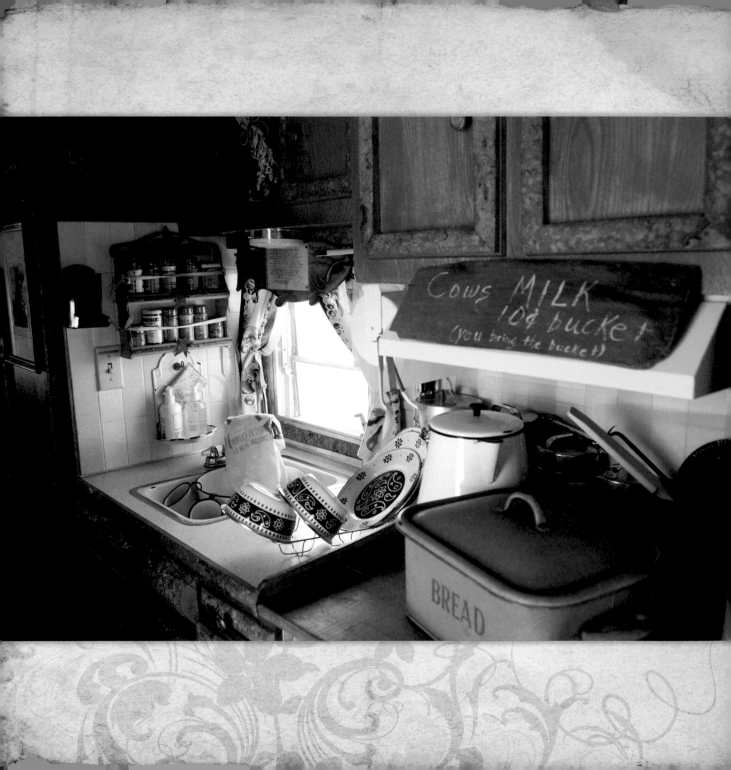

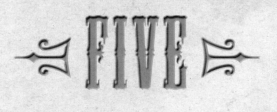

FIVE

WHAT TO TAKE ALONG

WHAT YOUR TRAILER NEEDS

Every trailer needs good bedding, and some of the finest linen was made in Ireland in the early twentieth century. Double-bed sheets are just the right size for most trailer beds and can be readily found and cheaply bought in antiques shops and thrift stores. Why? Because the old-fashioned double bed has fallen out of favor and been replaced by queen- and king-sized beds. For blankets, scour the tag sales and you'll find cotton Beacon blankets and wool Pendleton blankets. Highly sought-after are Hudson's Bay Company's thick wool point blankets. It is popularly believed that the dark lines on the side of each blanket indicate its worth—in beaver skins, but they actually denote its size and weight.

Many vintage trailers have spent years sitting outdoors and have, almost certainly, served as shelter for field mice, so the Sisters

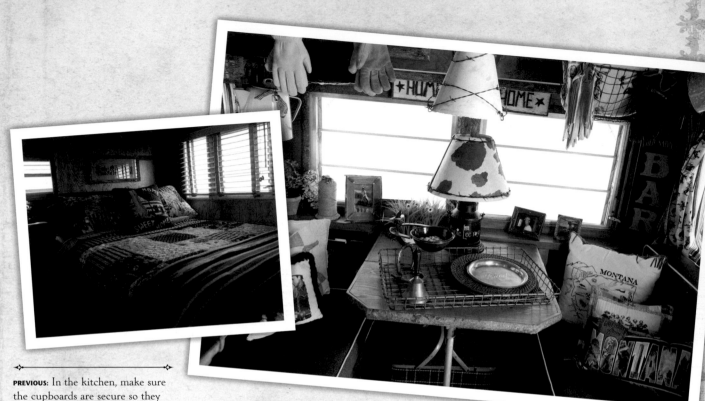

always make new dinette cushions. It is not difficult to make a knife-edge cushion—just measure the length, width, and depth and add half an inch for the seams. You might want to include a zipper, so the cushion cover can be removed for easy washing. For the seats, select a comfortable pad, measure the fabric, and, using a staple gun, staple the fabric to the wooden back of the seat bottoms.

Your camp kitchen will need pots and pans, dishes, glasses, and eating utensils. Cast-iron skillets and Dutch ovens are the most reliable and durable for cooking, and can readily be found in antiques malls. Look for the Griswold, Wagner, Wapak, Victor, or Erie markings, usually stamped right on the bottom. Because they won't break, painted tinware or vintage aluminum plates, bowls, and mugs are both a pretty and a practical choice. Stainless steel cutlery is the safest to use and easiest to clean. Many Sisters use cloth napkins for both aesthetic and ecological reasons. You can get heirloom napkins at thrift stores and church bazaars, and can sometimes even find thick damask napkins with monograms (never-used wedding gifts?).

Becky Clarke (Sister #2) suggests plastic plates: "Something nonbreakable because the cupboard doors always fly open." Don't forget a cute bucket for the sink "to become the pasta bucket or if you need a big bowl for salad . . . or even for washing up." During the drive, "You can store lanterns and lights in the bucket so they won't break."

If you're camping in a place with electrical hookups, take a tiny electric coffeepot. Grind your coffee, set everything up the night before, and whoever hits the floor first pushes the button. "Having fresh coffee first thing in the morning keeps people from getting grumpy," says Becky.

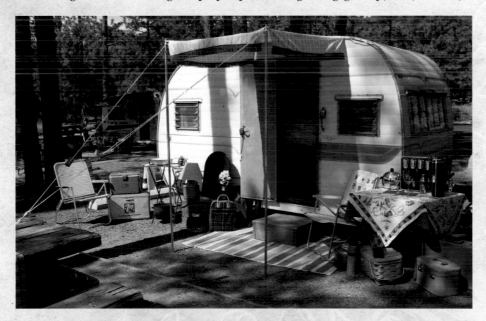

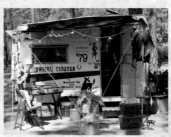

LEFT: Creating vignettes with flea market finds gives the Sisters a chance to show off their creative sides.

BELOW: The Sisters bring along all the collectibles—both useful and cute—they can fit in their trailers. And they enjoy every single piece.

Tools for the Trip

Must-Have Emergency Equipment

First-aid kit ✳ Cell phone ✳ Road flares ✳ Flashlight and plenty of batteries ✳ Basic set of tools—screwdrivers, pliers, wrenches ✳ Car jack and spare tire for all vehicles—car/truck and trailer ✳ Pocketknife and camping knife ✳ Small shovel ✳ Water and snacks ✳ Blanket for each individual ✳ Change of clothes ✳ Waterproof matches or fire starter ✳ Whistle and mirror (for signaling rescue crews)

Camping Equipment That Makes for a Pleasant Trip

Bedding ✳ Folding chairs and table ✳ Plastic tarp ✳ Duct tape ✳ Lantern, plus fuel or batteries ✳ Kitty litter or sand (to clean up spills or provide traction for tires) ✳ Trash bags ✳ Rope and clothespins ✳ Binoculars ✳ Compass or GPS ✳ Portable radio, either hand-crank or battery-powered ✳ Scissors ✳ Hammer ✳ Camping saw or hatchet ✳ Water filters ✳ Water bottle ✳ Camp stove fuel ✳ Aluminum foil ✳ Salt and pepper, herbs and spices ✳ Pots, pans, coffee, and/or teapot ✳ Cooler ✳ Can and bottle opener ✳ Corkscrew ✳ Kitchen knives ✳ Plastic spoons, knives, and forks ✳ Mugs and cups ✳ Plates and bowls (Becky suggests plastic or enamel) ✳ Plastic cutting board ✳ Spatula and tongs ✳ Hot pad ✳ Dishpan ✳ Sponge and dish towels ✳ Biodegradable soap ✳ Sandwich bags ✳ Food storage bags or containers ✳ Insect repellant ✳ Sunscreen ✳ Antiseptic wipes ✳ Antibiotic cream ✳ Burn ointment ✳ Lip balm ✳ Toothbrush and toothpaste ✳ Shampoo ✳ Soap ✳ Towel ✳ Toilet paper ✳ Weather-appropriate clothes, jackets, hats, and gloves

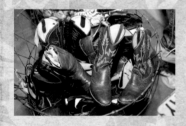

A Sister can never have too many pairs of cowgirl boots—some to keep, some to trade, some to loan out to other Sisters.

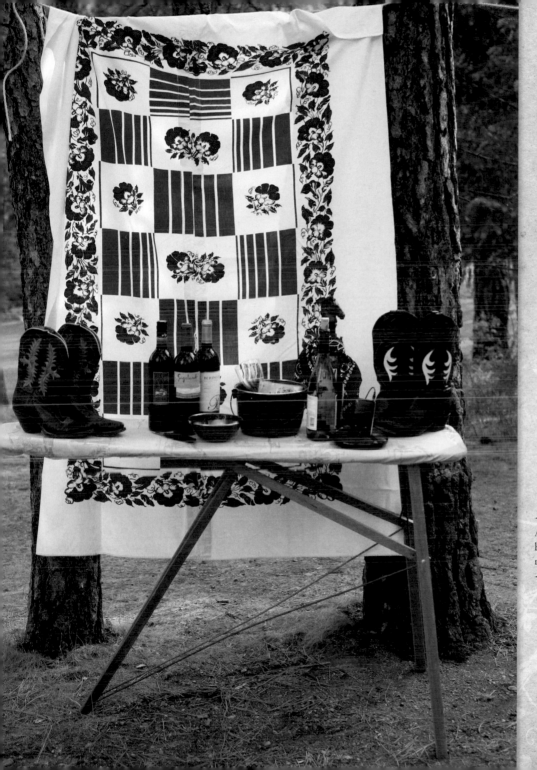

A vintage wooden ironing board becomes a wine and cheese bar in a matter of minutes.

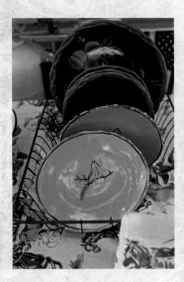

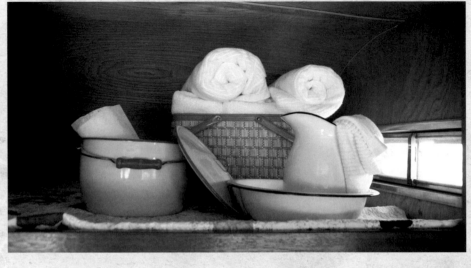

ABOVE: No paper plates for these gals. The Sisters enjoy their meals on kitschy plastic or pretty ceramic plates that match the overall themes of their trailers.

ABOVE RIGHT: Vintage enamelware does double duty—as storage for towels and washcloths and to use for washing up at day's end.

Many Sisters don't cook inside their trailers, preferring to cook outdoors on a camp stove or over a campfire. Even the Sisters who cook indoors will advise you not to cook bacon or fry fish inside your trailer, because the smell will linger forever. Since she rarely cooks inside her trailer, Becky uses her oven to store enamel mixing bowls, measuring cups, and larger pots. A heater and fan fit neatly under the seats in the dinette.

What's the last thing to put into your trailer before you get on the road? Folding chairs, a folding table, and a little rug to put in front of your door when you find the perfect camping spot. (It keeps you from tracking dirt and leaves into your trailer.)

More Must-Haves: Real Suggestions from Real Sisters
Battery-operated milk frother—for making the perfect cappuccino
Battery-operated blender—to make margaritas
Electric teapot

Coffee press
Cute cowgirl pajamas
All of your cowgirl boots—so everyone can try them on
A guest book
Vintage train cases—they're pretty and can hold/hide just about anything
Portable drill (fully charged)
Lots of duct tape
Extra taillight bulbs
Wooden ironing board (makes a great bar)
An extra set of keys (for your car and your trailer)
Heavy-duty extension cords (they are usually orange)
Extra sheets
Portable potty
Home fragrance spray (in case you forget to empty your potty)
A little gift for the event's hostess

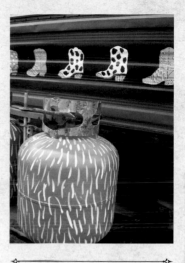

Trailer decor doesn't end with the interior and exterior. With some paint and lots of imagination, Amy Nicely (Sister #486) disguises her two propane tanks as barrel cacti.

WHAT TO LEAVE AT HOME

Becky says to pare down a little, especially if you're traveling with another Sister and space is at a premium. "If you have fishing books and camping books, leave those because there is not enough room, and who's going to have time to read anyway?" says Becky. She also suggests leaving behind half of your cute collectibles. Forget those cute extra throw pillows; they just get in the way. Leave your complete collection of state-shaped ashtrays; no one smokes anymore. Don't bring your favorite china or glassware because it could end up on the floor of your trailer—broken. Of course, most Sisters ignore this advice and bring all their cute stuff along to be traded and admired by the other Sisters.

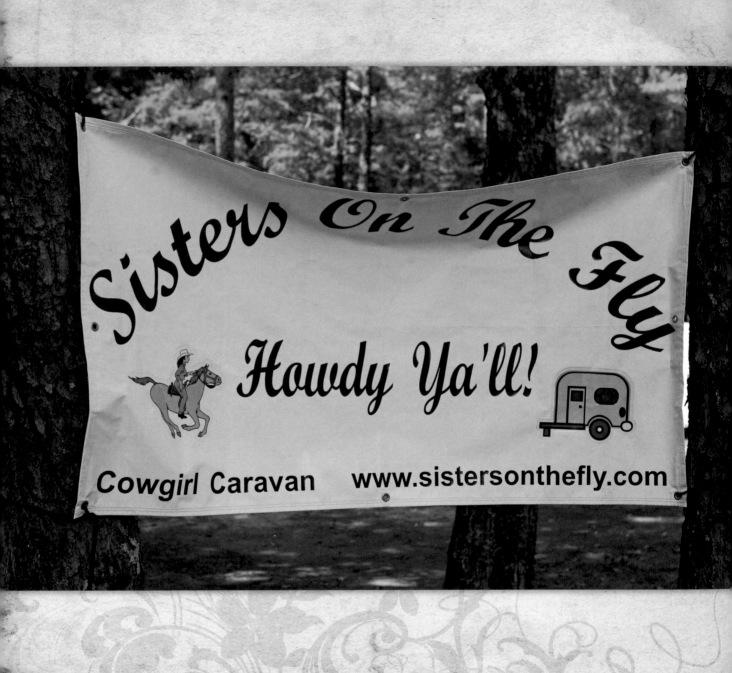

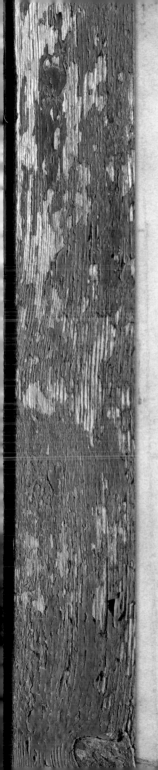

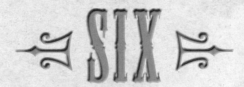

HOW WE GET TOGETHER

COWGIRL COLLEGE

In June every year, Maurrie and Becky organize an adventure that has nothing to do with fishing and everything to do with being a cowgirl. They host a group of ten women at Willow Creek Ranch in Kaycee, Wyoming, where they ride, rope, and brand for four days. It is at a spot made famous by Butch Cassidy and the Sundance Kid: Hole-in-the-Wall. The name refers to both the wide green valley where gang members pastured their rustled cattle and to the narrow trail through the high red-rock formation that forms part of the ranch's boundary. This precarious trail is still the only way to get into the valley from the east.

"It really is a hole, kind of a narrow trail, in a rock formation," says Maurrie. The outlaw period in the American West—romanticized by Louis L'Amour novels and John Wayne movies—lasted only

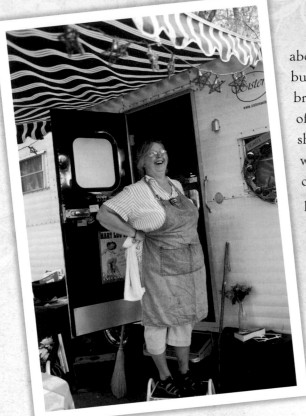

about thirty years (from 1875 to 1905), but the cattle rustlers, train robbers, brave lawmen, and lonesome cowboys of this era are still legendary. In those short decades when the West was truly wild—before it was finally fenced by the cattle ranchers—the Hole-in-the-Wall provided refuge to gunmen such as Jesse James and Butch Cassidy's Wild Bunch.

Today, Sisters stay in bunkhouses, eat in the kitchen with the ranch hands (yes, there have been some romances—everyone loves a cowboy), and ride the outlaw trail. "It is a working ranch," says Maurrie. "We are happy to get invited at branding time, which also happens to be my birthday. So I celebrate my birthday where I want to be—with my Sisters on horseback in the middle of nowhere."

GRANNIES ON THE LOOSE

Several years ago, Becky Clarke (Sister #2), Vickie Stoppello (Sister #5), and Ferne Krumm (Sister #28) decided to take their grandchildren (all about the same age) camping. "We needed to get them out of the city and into the forest," says Becky.

The first trip was to Idaho's Salmon River. "It was spawning time and the fish were like big old slugs, and the kids were screaming maniacs. It has taken a few years for us to teach them how to go about camping." The trick is to keep all the grandchildren busy "so they don't get into mischief."

One year they made tepees, combining woodcraft with a lesson in Native American history. Big kids teamed up with little kids to go out into the woods, find "the right kind" of poles, and lash them together. The Grannies thoughtfully provided canvas, paints, and a book on symbolism in Native American art and artifacts.

Last year, the Grannies camped on a small lake, so the project was boat making. Teams of four (two big ones and two little ones) created boats out of large pieces of cardboard (the kind that washing machines and refrigerators are delivered in—fortunately, most of the Grannies

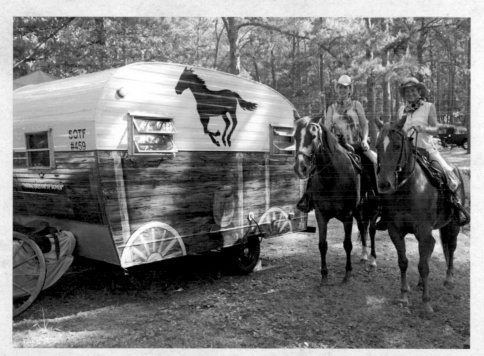

LEFT: The Southern Sisters are not so much into fly-fishing, but they ride. Decked out in cowgirl boots and hats, two Sisters head out for a leisurely ride through Alabama's piney woods.

BELOW: Kris Woody (Sister #30) bought a 1965 Caravel Airstream on her fiftieth birthday, named it Bob after her dad, and decorates it with bouquets of fresh flowers at every Sisters event.

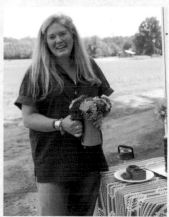

drive pickup trucks), miles and miles of duct tape, and paint to decorate the finished vessels.

"Each of the boats had to be floatable with two little kids in it," says Becky. "We had a start and finish line . . . not a great distance and all in shallow water. Surprisingly, two of the boats made it across the finish line."

Grannies on the Loose has grown from the original three grandmothers to include dozens more Sisters who want to spend quality time with their grandchildren away from the material distractions of city life. An additional and much-hoped-for benefit is that the younger generation will someday take over the travels and traditions of Sisters on the Fly.

SOUTHERN FRIED GOOD TIME

"The Southern Sisters are less about fishing and horses (although some of us do ride) than they are sitting down with a cup of coffee and getting to know you," says Anita Wallace (Sister #440), who organizes the Southern Fried Good Time, an annual campout that attracts Sisters from up and down the East Coast and even from as far away as New Jersey and Illinois.

To help those Northern Sisters fit right in, Anita prints out a flyer titled *How to Speak Southern*. It includes such phrases as "chewin' the fat" (talking about nothing), "hissy fit" (you don't have 'em, you pitch 'em), and the proper use of "Bless your heart" (before or after you say something that's "just a little bit" negative). She also includes a primer on Southern cooking—lots of butter, fatback, and lard; grits; collard greens; pulled-pork barbecue; pickled watermelon rinds; and, of course, gallons of sweet iced tea. She ends it with "See you soon—Lord willin' and the creek don't rise." Everyone smiles and knows exactly what she means.

Everywhere the Southern Sisters go, they "stage" their trailers and organize a trailer tour ("like a home tour, except with trailers") for a local charity. The Sisters recently raised $3,000 for a school in Savannah, Georgia, which, at $12 a pop, is a pretty impressive home tour by anyone's reckoning. "You spend all this time decorating your trailer and your family is probably pretty sick of hearing about it," Anita says. "This is like having a fan club, and you're the star of it." And, in most cases, a woman or two from the community will want to become a Sister.

Anita also organizes the Chattahoochee River Campout, one of the few trips that include husbands. "They help and encourage us. They do a lot of work on the old trailers we buy, making sure they are roadworthy. I think they deserve to be part of the fun," says Anita, who, in honor of the men, books a local bluegrass band for dancing.

SYNCHRONIZED FIREFLIES IN THE SMOKIES

For a few weeks in June, the fireflies in the Smoky Mountains do a magical thing. They put on a synchronized light show like nowhere on earth. They were "discovered" in the 1990s by a tourist who went up to a park ranger and complimented him on the "fabulous light show you put on last night." The ranger was puzzled but investigated and discovered that, in an area called Elkmont (once a summer retreat for upper-middle-class families from nearby Knoxville and Nashville, but now mostly in disrepair), thousands of fireflies were twinkling and blinking like Christmas lights.

Sharon Lambert (Sister #508) organizes an annual Sisters trip to see the fireflies. "We camp nearby and walk to the Elkmont cabins at night. One of the locals told us that the best place for 'firefly spotting' is the small cemetery, so we go there," she says. "We are totally surrounded by fireflies, they even land on us. I feel like I'm in the middle of a snow globe."

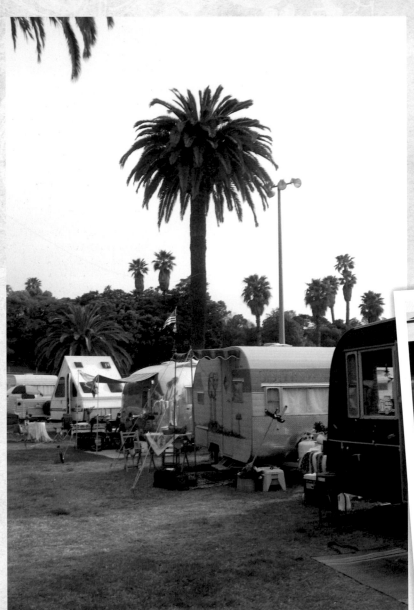

This magical show goes on every night from about 10 p.m. until 2 a.m., when all the "lights" go off and it becomes pitch-black. "We always carry flashlights to illuminate the road home," says Sharon, who also organizes the Saddle-Up in Pigeon Forge, Tennessee, and takes her trompe l'oeil log-cabin trailer to the National Cornbread Festival in South Pittsburg, Tennessee.

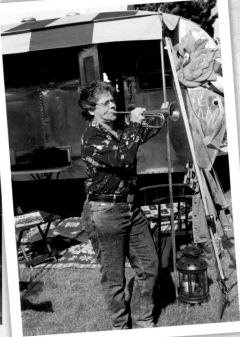

CALIFORNIA DREAMIN'

On a bluebird sunny day with a few high clouds and a little wind off the Pacific Ocean, more than sixty Sisters pull their trailers through the Spanish Mission–style gates into the Ventura County Fairgrounds. Major Molly Westgate (Sister #190 and, yes, she's a real U.S. Army major, now retired) and Tani Gibson (Sister #120) soon have the Sisters' trailers lined up in neat rows on the grass. "Just like a real neighborhood," says Molly, who travels with her bugle. She plays quite an accomplished reveille—adding lots of swirls and flourishes—and, as long as it is not too too early, the Sisters don't mind.

Some of the trailers are "cowgirled up," with larger than life murals of heroic women, painted ponies, and Mexican cantinas. Others are as highly polished as powder room mirrors. This is one of the bigger events, and Sisters can look forward to several days of antiquing (there's even a swap meet at the fairgrounds), museum going in Santa Barbara, and, of course, surf fishing—a first for some Sisters.

All the events were organized by California girls Kaarin Simpson (Sister #441) and Carol Sacher (Sister #328). Because this is one of the bigger campouts, they enlisted the help of Margo Warner (Sister #593), Joyce LaDuke (Sister #425), and Dale Gaberson (Sister #494). At day's end the Sisters return to

OPPOSITE LEFT: California Dreamin' saw the Sisters' trailers lined up in neat rows, like a little neighborhood.

OPPOSITE RIGHT: Major Molly Westgate (Sister #190) rouses the Sisters for a day of surf fishing and antiquing in nearby Santa Barbara.

BELOW RIGHT: On the step of her 1958 Westerner, Janet Castagnola (Sister #511), in sunglasses and fuzzy bathrobe, offers the Sisters a cup of her fresh, strong coffee.

BELOW: At the Farm Chicks gathering, Grace Brown (Sister #473) shows off the hand sewn banner that travels to all Sisters events in the Pacific Northwest.

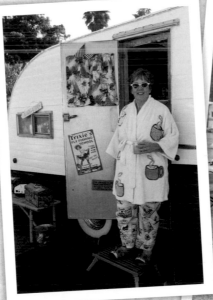

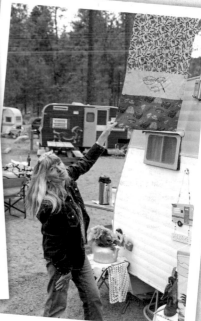

their vintage trailer neighborhood for a potluck dinner, a trailer trash–themed party (everyone shows up in fuzzy leopard prints and big plastic sunglasses), and music under the stars.

Some of the more energetic Sisters walk along the beach and come back with armloads of seashells—to be turned into crafts by the more artistic Sisters. School librarian Peggy Burns (Sister #229) says being a Sister "takes me out of my personal box and widens my world."

GIDDY DOWN

When some of the Texas Sisters couldn't take time off work to attend California Dreamin', they organized a trip of their own in a tiny campground called the Grapevine in Grapevine, Texas. Organizer Cathy Preston (Sister #510) was surprised at the great response. "It was filled up and had a waiting list in two days."

Because all the Texas Sisters have "a little cowgirl in them," one of the trip's high points was a visit to the National Cowgirl Museum and Hall of Fame in Fort Worth, Texas. The rest of the trip featured great garage sales, visiting the quaint little shops on Grapevine's main street, learning to line dance at Billy Bob's, and buying a "SOTF (Sisters on the Fly) tree" to plant in the campground. Despite all the activity, Cathy doesn't like to jam-pack the days.

"We want to have enough time to just sit and talk," she says. "The Sisters are some of the best friends I've ever known. It is hard to explain to someone the camaraderie we have." She talks about one Giddy Down when it rained and rained and the nearby Dallas Cowboys facility was blown away by tornadoes. "Picture this: Fifteen Sisters in pajamas and galoshes, crammed into one of those sturdy brick women's bathrooms. We laughed and had fun, waiting for the storm to blow by," she says. At the beginning of a trip, the Sisters may be complete strangers, but by the end, "You have a sister, someone you can call on."

FARM CHICKS

It used to be that, every spring, farm women in the Spokane, Washington, area would hold weekly garage sales, selling antiques, collectibles, produce, and farm-fresh eggs at the ends of their farm driveways. They called themselves "the farm chicks." Now, the Farm Chicks has an entirely new meaning. Serena Thompson, cofounder of the Farm Chicks, says, "A Farm Chick loves her family, laughs a lot, and sees the world through rose-colored glasses."

Annually, in June, Serena produces one of the country's coolest antiques shows—featuring country objects, cowgirl collectibles, and plenty of shabby chic. Grace Brown (Sister #473) organized a Sisters on the Fly meet-and-fish to take place at the same time as the Farm Chicks antiques show. Tammy Fuller (Sister #113) shares a booth full of kitchen antiques, vintage linens, birdhouses, and other collectibles at the show with her daughter, Emily Schreiner (Sister #968).

The Sisters arrive at the antiques show early and shop hard, eager to bag the best treasures to show off "back at

When a Sister finally admits to having too much stuff, she has a sale. Here Tammy Fuller (Sister #113) and her daughter, Emily Schreiner (Sister #968), pose in their booth at the Farm Chicks antiques show with Farm Chicks cofounders Teri Edwards and Serena Thompson.

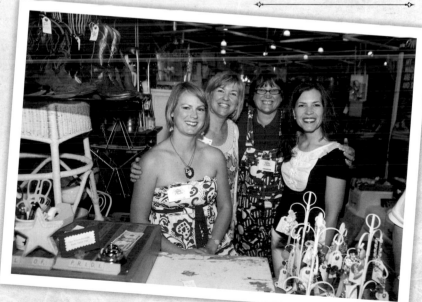

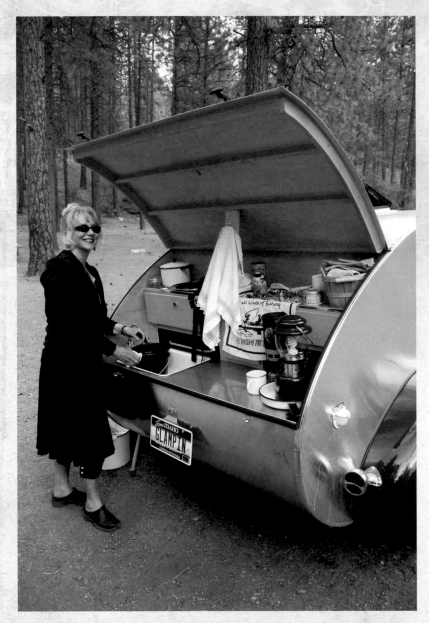

the ranch." Jani Sharp (Sister #450) says, "There's nothing old in my house, so every collectible I buy has to fit into my trailer."

MaryJane Butters (Sister #1315) of MaryJanesFarm joins the Sisters to show off one of her brand-new teardrop trailers. "Originally, I designed this for Robert Redford," she says. Now, she's selling them on the MaryJanesFarm Web site. At only seven hundred pounds, they are great starter trailers for women not comfortable pulling larger, heavier trailers.

COWGIRL CARAVAN EVENTS

Many of the Sisters organize individual Cowgirl Caravan events, tailored to suit the Sisters in their parts of the country. Melanie Brown (Sister #903) has a Cow Paddy Campout in her pasture (no hookups—only Porta Potti toilets) that's bordered by the Snake River in Glenns Ferry, Idaho. Janine Pettit (Sister #563) invites Sisters

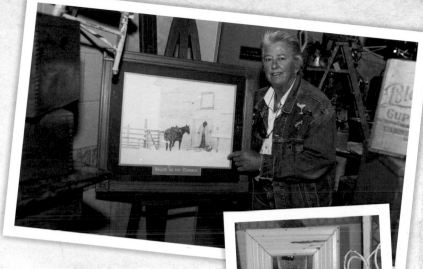

to a "farm girl camp" on her six-acre hobby farm in rural New Jersey for camping, crafts, and collecting eggs from her designer chickens. The Caney Cove Camp-O-Rama is organized by Rhoni Fields (Sister #625), Cheryl Tanner (Sister #796), and Linda Brede (Sister #250) and includes fishing on Cedar Creek Lake "off the dock or out of any one of the local Sisters' boats" and antiquing in the little towns all around Malakoff, Texas.

Fishing out of canoes and lots of Dutch oven cooking (including a demonstration by a local Dutch oven master) are highlights of the White Buffalo Roundup in Mountain Home, Arkansas. Organizer Cheri McDonald (Sister #802), who has seventeen cast-iron pots, cooks up her Scottish grandmother's shepherd's pie (recipe in chapter 8) in her antique Dutch oven.

Cowgirl Finishing School takes place on Jane Bishoff's (Sister #295) ranch in way-southern Arizona, near the Mexico border. Sisters learn rope tricks, write cowgirl poetry, and dress like *Gunsmoke*'s Miss Kitty to attend the Lonesome Dove Ball held at the reputedly haunted Copper Queen Hotel in Bisbee, Arizona.

When SalsaFest takes place in September in Safford, Arizona, Sisters on the Fly open up their trailers for touring and quickly become the talk of the town. Karla Jones (Sister #303) organizes the Chilly Chili Cuddle Up at her ranch in Broken Arrow, Oklahoma. Since the event is in January, she advises Sisters to "bring your generators, your long johns, and your sense of humor."

OPPOSITE: MaryJane Butters (Sister #1315) cooks dinner in the teardrop she originally designed for Robert Redford. She now makes and sells these designs at MaryJanesFarm.

TOP: Tani Gibson (Sister #120) looks at some art for her trailer at the Farm Chicks sale. "Let's not forget a salute to the cowgirls," she says.

BOTTOM: The Sisters' fabulous finds wait to be picked up and taken back to camp.

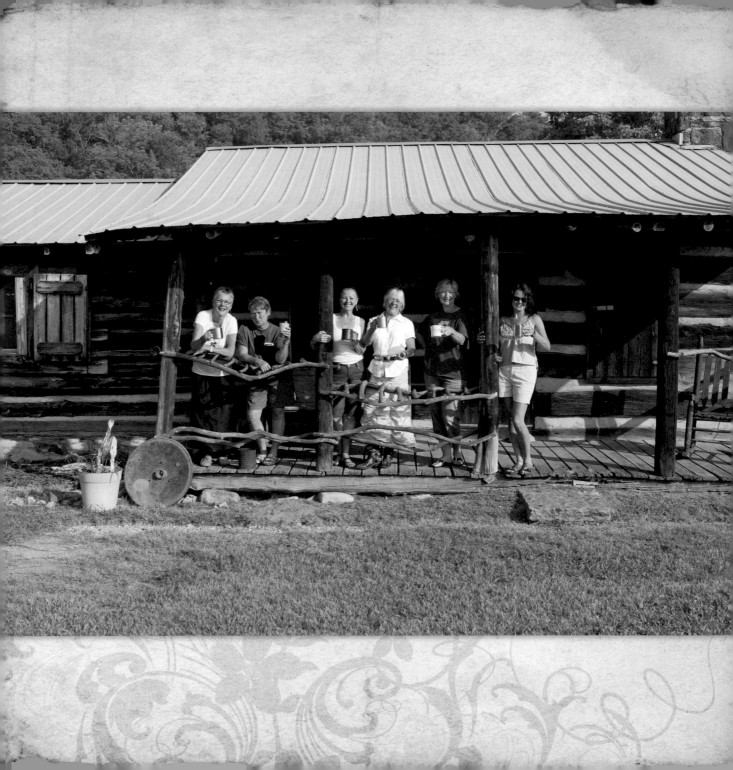

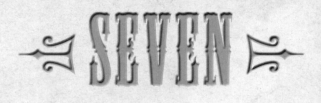

SEVEN

THE JOYS OF SISTERHOOD

The Sisters have three rules: 1) No husbands, 2) No dogs, and 3) Be nice. The husbands rule is sometimes suspended (they are allowed to attend a few Sisters adventures), and sometimes dogs are allowed (when the girls are going riding instead of fishing), but the most important rule—"Be nice"—always holds true.

Like most women, Maurrie Sussman (Sister #1) is a caregiver and a pillar of her family and her community. "We're always doing for other people—kids, husbands, parents—and not spending much time on ourselves," says Maurrie, who looks at the Sisters' adventures as a temporary escape from her life as a wife, mother, and animal rescuer. So when she says "Be nice," she's also reminding you to be nice to yourself.

There are not many places where a woman can go to rediscover that little girl that's still inside of her, where she can be young again and act a little silly. There are not many people to whom she can say

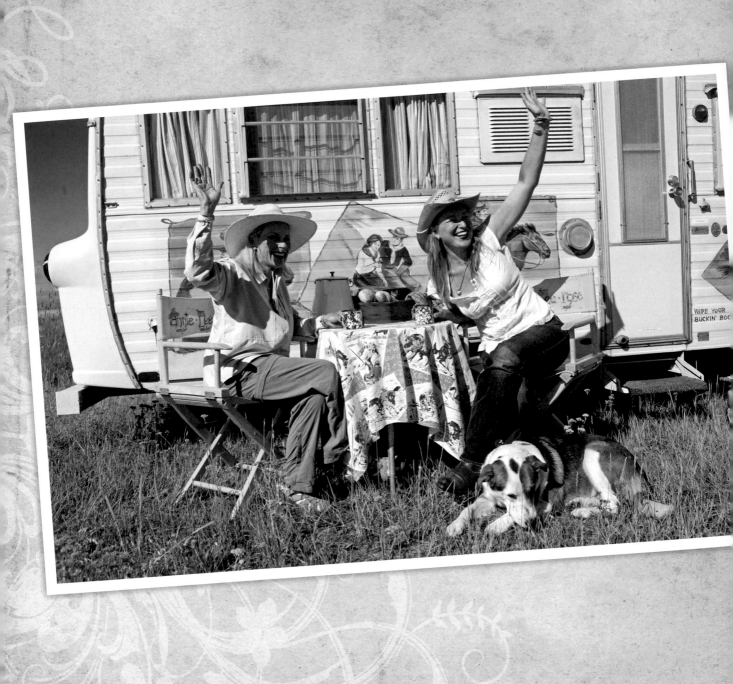

the things that she would never say to anyone, ever. For a few carefree days with her Sisters, a woman can be that little girl again. Sure, when they go home, they will turn back into judges, grandmothers, bank presidents, high school teachers, and accountants again, but for those few sunny days, life is simple and good.

SISTERS OF THE HEART

Early sisterhoods in the West were called "Cow belles" or extension clubs. Once a month, women from far-flung ranches and farms would gather at community halls or at one of their homes. Yes, they were official meetings with officers and duties, but one must wonder if that was just to keep their husbands from calling it a gossip group. There was some gossip, to be sure, but the meetings were mainly a chance for the women—minorities in a rough-and-tumble environment—to connect with one another.

They exchanged ideas on child rearing, traded recipes, and shared housekeeping tips. They compared notes on calving, the weather, and the price of wheat. It was a comfortable, wonderful place where news was gathered and passed on, and where women could shed their jeans and work boots, don skirts, put on lipstick, and feel like women. They could relax and reveal the gentle souls underneath their tough exteriors. They could connect and communicate with their own kind.

A sister of the heart doesn't come from your family and is not related by blood ties or lineage. Instead, she's someone with whom you have a connection that's deeper than friendship. She gives you a smile at the very moment when you need it most. She squeezes your hand unexpectedly when there are tears in your eyes, and frustration or grief is about to get the best of you. She overhears you telling someone that you love a certain

PREVIOUS: Mornings are a great time for planning the day's activities over a hot cup of coffee, but one of the Sisters makes sure the coffeepot is on all day.

OPPOSITE: Wherever Sisters gather, they can expect a warm welcome. Debra Bolnik (Sister #45) and Krista Cartwright (Sister #1296) wave to newly arriving Sisters.

kind of chocolate and, wow! a little box shows up in your mailbox without any explanation at all.

She hears through the grapevine that you've had a bad week and sends you a funny e-mail to say she is thinking of you. She doesn't need an explanation; she just reaches out to the ones she loves. She takes the time to send a note saying, quite simply, that she appreciates who you are and is grateful for your friendship. She hears the stress in your voice during a routine how-are-you phone call and asks how she can help.

Sisterhood can be demonstrated in an active group doing wonderful "together" things, as the Sisters on the Fly do with their fishing trips and Cowgirl Caravan events. It can also be shown in the way in which Sisters get together for lunch or long, tell-all phone calls—always with a level of understanding that is unique to women who are sisters of the heart.

Sisterhoods still exist in rural areas and are terrific morale boosters—places of joy and sharing that farm and ranch women looked forward to with anticipation. Today, even though rural areas are less remote because of technology, there are still areas where women are few and far between. In rural Montana, you can stop a rancher in a general store to ask about his wife and he'll reply, "She's baking and talking on the phone." They live thirty-five miles from the nearest highway. It is a long way to anywhere from their ranch, and that phone is her saving grace, her chance to talk to someone on those long lonely days when her husband is out in the fields. Imagine what it was like when there weren't any phones.

Sisters on the Fly fills just this kind of spiritual need in both urban and rural women: the need to be with sisters of the heart—women who understand that a woman can pull a calf as well as a man, that her gender doesn't determine whether she can drive a tractor, and her adeptness at running a chainsaw has no bearing on her ability to turn out an extraordinary soufflé.

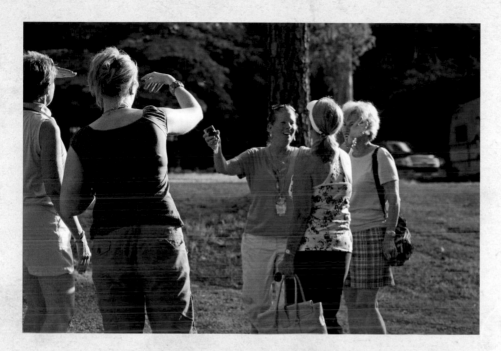

Sisters are both quiet and thoughtful and strong and resourceful. A Sister knows how to use baling wire to fix the zipper on her best dress when it breaks in the feed truck on the way to church. She knows how to change a tire on a dirt road in a snowstorm when cell service is just a pipe dream. She enjoys the silver song of quaking aspens, the whispery breeze through a mountain valley, the clarity of a stream, the song of a meadowlark, the yip of a coyote. She also enjoys heading into town in all her cowgirl finery—turquoise, velvet, leather, and lots of fringe.

Lifelong bonds form during the Sisters' grand adventures, fabulous meals, and lively conversations.

SISTERS FORM BONDS BY BEING COWGIRLS TOGETHER

The summer had been glorious and, on the mountains, the aspens were in their full fall regalia of burnished orange and yellow. No fishing today.

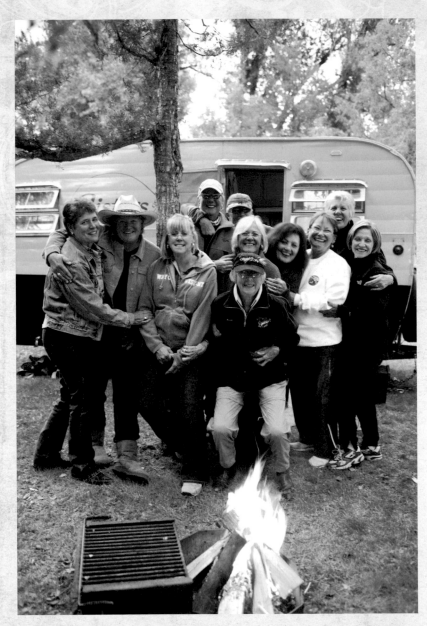

This warm day was devoted to rounding up pastured horses.

Horses caught, the Sisters decided a bareback ride back to the ranch was in order; the sun was shining brightly and the sky was clear. The weather in the West is fickle, however, and by the time the Sisters reached the cover of an aspen grove, it had started to rain.

Thinking the storm surely wouldn't last long, the Sisters decided to wait it out. But the longer they waited, the harder it rained. They had no choice but to get on and ride with their hat brims ducked to protect their faces from the driving rain. The only warmth came from the horses. The water dripped off their hats and ran down backs covered only in light summer jackets. Hands turned red from cold, and noses ran as they trotted on through sagebrush and meadows—not a tree in sight. After forty-five minutes in the driving rain, they made it to the barn, dripping, laughing, and soaked to the bone.

The horses were dry in only one spot, where they had carried Sisters on their backs. All the women needed to warm up were a good fire, a warm blanket, a hot cup of tea, or maybe a hot toddy. They quickly overcame the chilly adventure, but the story lives on.

AND SOMETIMES THEY JUST SIT AND TALK

The night is dark—like the bottom of an inkpot—with just a sliver of a moon peeking through the trees. There's not another light to be seen anywhere, but the Sisters' campfires burn brightly to ward off any ghosts or bears that might be lurking in the thickets that surround the campground. The night air is heavy with the smell of honeysuckle. Dinner dishes have been washed and put away. The Dutch oven jambalaya (recipe in chapter 8) was delicious. Wine glasses are filled. Voices swell with song and then become silent again as conversations pick up. All around the campfires Sisters are talking with Sisters, catching up with old friends and getting to know the newbies. When a Sister at one of the campfires tells a particularly good story, the others gather around. Some of these stories will eventually be circulated via e-mail to Sisters all across the country.

Here's one told last summer: One of the recently divorced Sisters had found the perfect dress

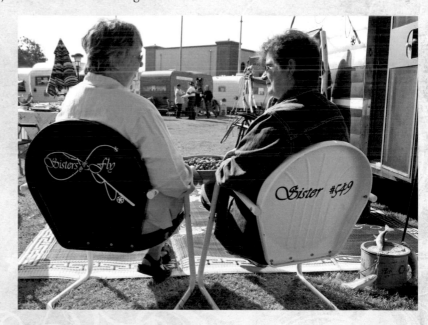

for her daughter's wedding. Her ex-husband would be attending with his new, much younger wife. The bride was horrified to discover that her new stepmother would be wearing the same dress. Asked politely, her stepmother refused to exchange the dress, so the bride's mother (the teller of this story) agreed to get another dress for the wedding. The bride and her mother went shopping and bought another gorgeous dress.

"So, when are you going to return dress number one?" asked the bride.

"Oh," said the mother, "I'm wearing it to the rehearsal dinner, the night before the wedding."

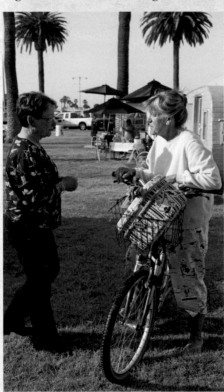

Sometimes the showers are too far to walk to, so Sisters use bikes for transportation. Those cute train cases are great for carrying shampoo and other shower necessities. Nancy Baum (Sister #697), on the bike, stops to chat with Kaarin Simpson (Sister #441).

Everyone laughs. Some, perhaps, in recognition of a similar situation. Is it true? Who knows? But it is part of the lore that binds the Sisters together.

Beverly Brand (Sister #615) works for the public school system in Chattanooga, Tennessee, and has a 1958 Serro Scotty. "The first time I went on a Sisters adventure, I signed on for only one night, just to see what the women were like." To her surprise and delight, she felt like she had always known this group of classy, sassy, smart, funny, independent women. "We have fun and don't spat as much as real sisters," she says.

A Tomboy Gets Lots of Sisters

Sisters . . . I never had one that was blood. My sisters were the women that I admired as I grew into an adult: the teachers and coaches that touched my life, 4-H leaders, and my grandmother.

One in particular was Pat. She was in high school when she took me under her wing. I was eight or nine. She taught me the finer points of showing cattle. She took me to shows, coached me, and listened to me as I struggled my way into being a teenager. When she went to college, she was still my sounding board about boys and rebellion, school and sports. She was a good listener and always gave solid advice. Way out in the boondocks, she was the closest thing I had to a real sister.

I grew up surrounded by men —my dad and my brother. I was as tomboy as you could get, but I was still a girl and they didn't seem to understand. Pat was a ranch girl, too, and I thought she was the most beautiful thing I had ever seen. She taught me about makeup and took me shopping for feminine clothes. I learned that girls can have horses, cows, and pickups, but they don't have to give up their feminine side. They can appreciate the outdoors, and when they find others who like the same things, they bond. This is a lesson I'm learning all over again from my Sisters on the Fly.

❖ *Thea Marx (Sister #1323)*

SISTERS ON THE FLY PATCHES

All of the Sisters have jean jackets or vests with patches sewn on them. Some have a lot of patches; some have just a few but wear them proudly. The patches started when Kathy Wolfe and Barb Verhage (they share Sister #10) said, "These adventures remind us of Girl Scouts, but we got patches back in the day." Maurrie was in a junk store and found some old Girl Scout books from the 1920s and saw that there were, indeed, cute patches for all kinds of amazing accomplishments. So Maurrie began designing patches appropriate to Sisters on the Fly.

The first one was a tiny trailer given to Sisters when they joined the group. The next patch was for making and serving the group's signature lemon drop martini (recipe in chapter 8). After that came the Purple Heart patch for anyone who got injured on a Sisters trip. Maurrie notes that while getting a bad splinter could merit receiving the patch, a broken nail just does not count toward a Purple Heart.

The Mazie patch came when Mazie was approaching ninety and everyone felt more comfortable if they paired her up for the day with another Sister—just in case Mazie fell and broke her hip. In reality, the Sisters earn the Mazie patch by huffing and puffing to keep up with her— especially when she's fishing or thrifting.

When one of the Sisters said she should get a patch for going potty outside, Maurrie designed one. After the hilarious time the Sisters had planning and attending Cowgirl Prom, Maurrie designed a patch that reflected the attire most of the Sisters wore—a pink prom dress from the 1960s with a cowgirl hat and boots.

The Rosie the Riveter patch is named after a World War II cultural icon representing the American women who worked in factories while the men were off at war. This patch is awarded to women who are handy with tools and who cheerfully come to the aid of their Sisters who are not.

A Naked Nymphs patch is awarded to women who take showers outdoors in the nude. "That patch came about after a fishing trip to the Navajo lands," explains Maurrie. "We were in a sweat lodge, modestly wrapped in towels, and afterward we were supposed to step out and stand under a cold outdoor shower. I've got to tell you, it is difficult to take a shower with a big towel wrapped around you. By this time, we were giggling so hard and we just threw down our towels and had a proper shower."

Some patches are funny and fun. Others are serious. Diversity (one high heel, one flat) is an important patch awarded to Sisters who show tolerance of the views of others. Helping Hands and Sisters in Need are patches that could be awarded over and over again, because whenever Sisters perceive a need, they step in to lend a hand or offer a shoulder to cry on.

In all, there are more than a dozen patches, and some Sisters have earned all of them. But Sisterhood is not about earning patches. It is about a bond that extends way beyond adventures, campfires, and caravans. One

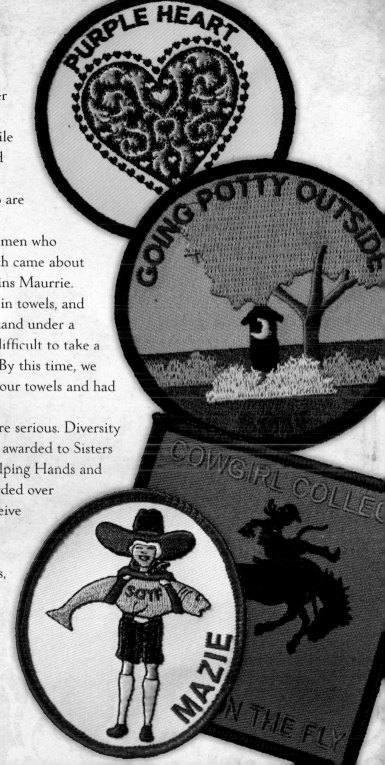

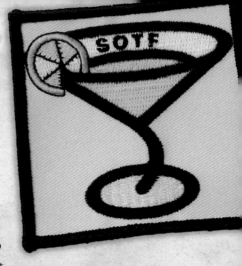

Sister tells how her college-aged son's car broke down on a cross-country trip. When he called, she looked up a Sister in the nearest town, and that's where he stayed while his car was being fixed.

Another Sister recounts the support she received when she was diagnosed with breast cancer. The Sisters made her a quilt "to keep her warm until she could rejoin them and get some real warm hugs." In fact, the Sisters have made dozens of patchwork quilts to send to Sisters who are sick, maybe undergoing chemo, or facing other life-challenging illnesses. Stories like this are not unique; they abound.

ALWAYS THERE FOR ONE ANOTHER

Sharon Lambert (Sister #508) recounts this story: When Hurricane Katrina was bearing down on New Orleans and the area was told to evacuate, Karen LeGlue (Sister #459), her mother, Leona (also a Sister), and her two daughters and their families were forced to leave their homes.

"I have a large old family home, now used just for vacations, in Mississippi, about two and a half hours from New Orleans, and we offered it to them," says Sharon.

While in Mississippi, Karen met Sharon's eighty-five-year-old aunt Joyce. Months later, after Aunt Joyce suffered a stroke, Karen and Leona traveled back up to Mississippi to "sit with" Aunt Joyce, because "that's what Sisters do."

A dear Sister (this one has to remain nameless and numberless) has a bad habit of marrying the wrong men. She chooses the same kind of guy over and over again, hoping, each time, the outcome will be different. The men she chooses are dazzling and dangerous. They wine and dine her and treat her like a princess until after the wedding. Twice she has called for help and, each time, a Sister has been there to step in. The good news is that our dear Sister is now dating someone nice and kind—not devilishly handsome but really cute.

And where there is life, there is always death. Sometimes it is a Sister succumbing to cancer after a long illness. Sometimes it's the death of a beloved aunt or, God forbid, a spouse. The Sisters always gather around (sometimes traveling great distances) to ease a fellow Sister's sorrow in the ways they know best— making a quilt, bringing a casserole, hugging, listening, and understanding.

And sometimes just sitting down—on the nearest available seat—is a good thing at the end of a long day. Christa Cartwright (Sister #1296) sits and contemplates the joys of Sisterhood.

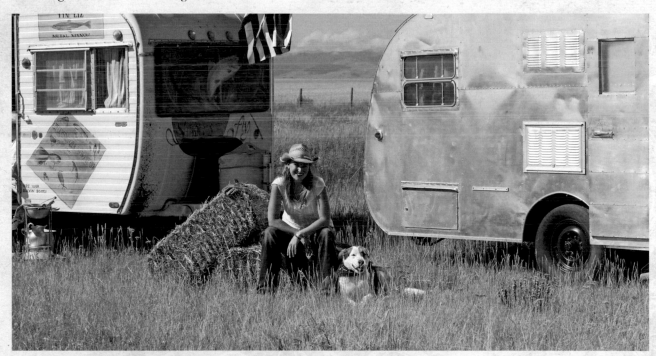

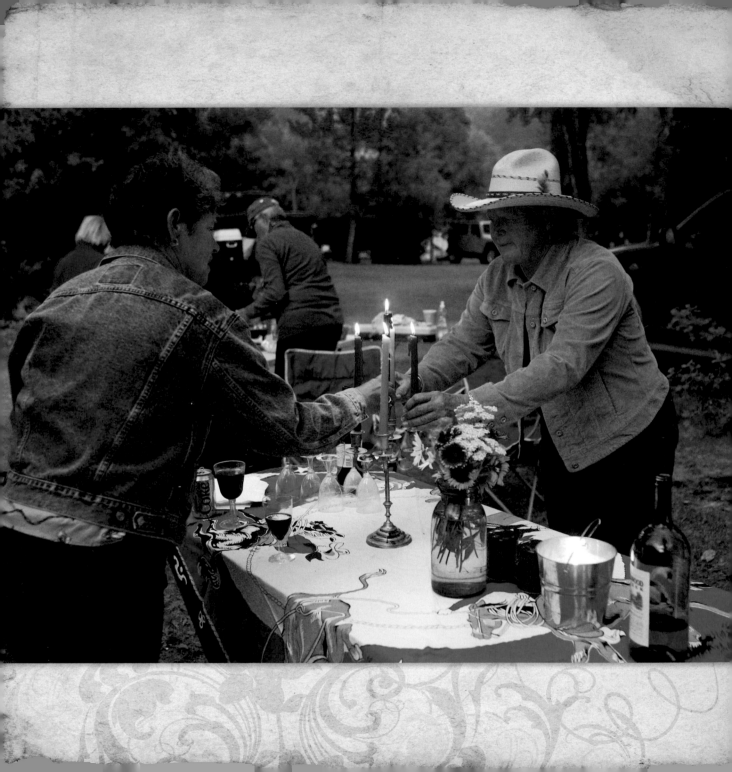

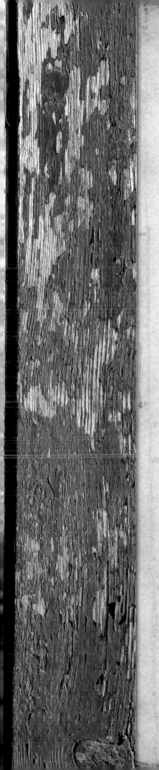

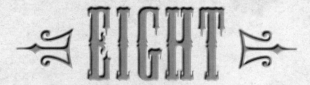

AROUND THE CAMPFIRE

After a long day of fishing (or bargaining at the antiques shops), the Sisters gather around the campfire to have a glass of wine, cook dinner, share recipes, and tell stories.

They clear the picnic tables and toss cowgirl-themed tablecloths across them—not straight across, but on the diagonal. Someone brings out tall silver candlesticks that gleam in the firelight. Citronella candles smoke their lemony mosquito repellent. Dinner, cooking over the campfire, is beginning to smell good. The sun is low and amber in the western sky as the Sisters sit down to eat food that is simple and delicious in the way that food cooked and eaten out-of-doors always is.

For most Sisters, food is love. That love is represented by finding and perfecting recipes to cook over the campfire and share with other Sisters. Some are family recipes, enjoyed by Grandma and Grandpa in the early days of trailer travel before the interstate highway system made it easy to get to today's popular camping spots in the national parks and along good-fishing rivers such as the Yellowstone and the Colorado. Some come from now-out-of-print cookbooks; some from the Internet. No matter where the recipe comes from, the campfire food is cooked to perfection, served with a flourish, and garnished with love.

DUTCH OVEN DIVAS

Many of the Sisters are really into Dutch oven cooking. They light charcoal briquettes in the campfire and then transfer them to the edge of the fire ring, away from the flames, to create a more even heat by placing just the right number of briquettes below the Dutch oven and on the lid. For dinner, it's chili cornbread pie; for dessert, blackberry cobbler made with freshly picked berries. In the morning, they'll use the Dutch oven lids to cook pancakes and eggs.

PREVIOUS: Sisters don't let their rough, rugged surroundings affect the dinner preparations; table linens, candles, and fresh flowers are always part of a properly set table.

BELOW: Chow time: The Sisters know how to put on a spread, complete with long-trusted recipes, fresh produce, and, of course, an interesting variety of local wines.

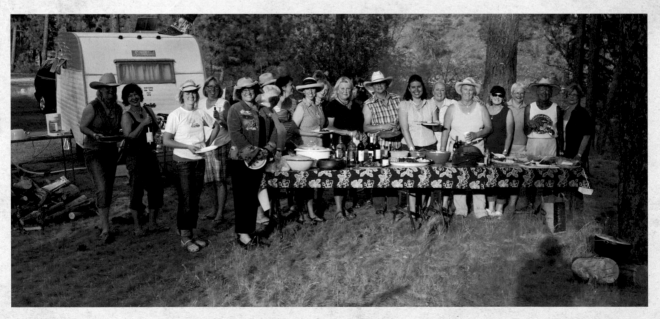

The Dutch Oven Divas of the Desert meet every January near Quartzite, Arizona, where they show off their Dutch oven culinary skills. "Last year more than fifty women and their trailers showed up for the event," says Babs Schmitt (Sister #90), who organizes this annual event.

For the faithful, anything less durable than cast iron just won't do. Although they are not exactly pretty, cast-iron skillets and Dutch ovens (sometimes called camp ovens) have many virtues, which the Sisters are quick to enumerate. For one, cast iron is heavy—so you don't need to go to the gym as often. It lasts forever and you can pass it on to your grandchildren. It has a natural nonstick surface, and the more you cook in it, the better it cooks.

A cast-iron Dutch oven has enormous versatility. If you take it camping, you can cook every single meal in it. You can use it to deep fry, braise, or simmer a stew or chili. Nothing sears a steak as well as cast iron. It cleans up with a little warm water and a scrub brush. For difficult cooked-on food, the Sisters suggest a light scrubbing with a paste of coarse salt and water . . . and that takes care of it. Rust is the sworn enemy of cast iron; dry your cast iron thoroughly after washing. The best way is to simply put it on the ashes of a nearly burned-out campfire and let it dry naturally.

An often-repeated cooking tip: Don't use lighter fluid to light your charcoal briquettes or anything you cook in your Dutch ovens will taste of lighter fluid.

Sisters swear by the well-worn Griswold ovens handed down from their grandmothers. They can still be found in antiques shops for between $80 and $100. New cast-iron pots, made by the family-owned Lodge Manufacturing Company in South Pittsburg, Tennessee, cost about the same as the antiques.

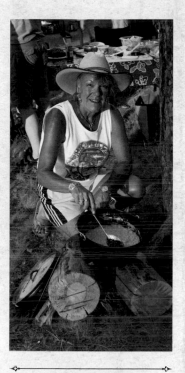

Nancy Baum (Sister #697) cooks up a batch of stick-to-your-ribs grits for the group in her trusty Dutch oven.

Lodge, founded in 1896, is the sole remaining cast-iron cookware manufacturer in the United States. The company sponsors the National Cornbread Festival (annually in April) and offers hundreds of Dutch oven recipes on its Web site (http://www.lodgemfg.com), including this prize winner made by the ladies of the First Baptist Church for the 2009 National Cornbread Festival.

Smoked Sausage and Hot Water Corn Cakes

These hearty cakes mix up quickly and can be served with a salad for an easy lunch or wrapped up as a snack for an afternoon hike.

Makes 20 to 25 cakes.

Enough vegetable oil to fill a Dutch oven 1 1/2 inches deep
1 1/2 cups white self-rising cornmeal
1 1/2 cups self-rising flour
1 tablespoon sugar
3 cups water, boiling
2 eggs, slightly beaten
1 cup chopped onions
1 cup cubed smoked sausage
1 small jar pimentos, mashed

Heat the oil in a Dutch oven over a charcoal fire until it is very hot (about 400°F). In a large bowl, combine the cornmeal, flour, and sugar. Pour the boiling water into the dry mixture and stir until sticky. Fold the eggs into the mixture. Add the onions, sausage, and pimentos and stir well. Using a large cooking spoon, drop spoonfuls of dough into the hot cooking oil. Turn cakes two or three times to brown evenly. Place on paper towels to drain.

Dutch Oven Breakfast

Glenda (G!) Stone (Sister #62) likes to serve this with warm flour tortillas and her favorite salsa. Vegetables such as peppers or mushrooms can be added at the same time as the onions.

Serves 8.

> 8 eggs
> 1/4 cup milk
> 2 pounds sausage
> 1 medium yellow onion, diced
> 2 pounds potatoes, grated
> 2 cups grated cheese (any yellow cheese is good)

In a bowl, mix together the eggs and milk and set aside. Brown the sausage and onion in a 12-inch or 14-inch Dutch oven. Remove, and brown the potatoes in the sausage grease. (If you are using turkey or low-fat sausage, add 2 tablespoons of canola oil.) After the potatoes are browned, return the sausage and onions to the oven and stir. Add the egg mixture and stir. Cover with a lid, and put 12 hot briquettes on top. Bake for 20 minutes or until the eggs are done. Remove cover and add cheese. Continue baking until cheese is melted.

Breakfast Casserole

Kim Korstad (Sister #373) says this recipe is great for camping. She makes it up early in the morning, goes fishing, comes back, and has a Ramos Fizz while it is baking.

Serves 8

10 slices or whole loaf of bread (cut off crusts and pull apart into bite-size pieces)
1 pound bacon, cooked well and crumbled
2 cups grated cheddar cheese
6 green onions, chopped
7 eggs, lightly beaten
3 to 4 cups milk (enough to make the mixture very moist)
Salt and pepper

Combine all the ingredients and let soak for at least one hour before baking. Spoon the mixture into a Dutch oven, cover with a lid, and place 12 hot briquettes on top. Bake for 20 to 30 minutes until done. Let stand for 10 to 15 minutes before cutting and serving.

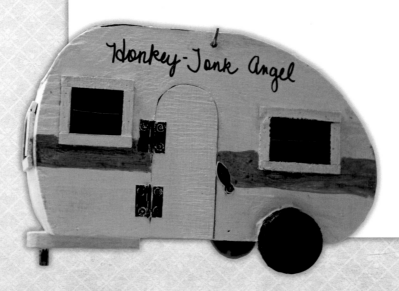

Fish Chowder

"This is a recipe given to me by an old-timer, and I really love it. It is quick, easy, and perfect for store-bought fish or the catch of the day." —Rene Knopp Groom (Sister #1281)

Serves 6

- 1 package of pork bacon, cut into small pieces
- 2 sweet onions, sliced
- 3 potatoes, diced
- 1 quart water
- 6 fish fillets, cut in 1-inch pieces
- 1 (13-ounce) can evaporated milk
- 1 teaspoon salt
- Generous pinch of freshly ground black pepper
- 1 tablespoon butter or margarine

Warm your Dutch oven on a stove or over a campfire to about 350°F. Brown the bacon, and then add the onions and potatoes to brown in the bacon grease. Add the water and simmer for 10 minutes. Add the fish and simmer for 5 minutes. Add the milk, salt, and pepper and top with butter at the last minute. Serve with good bread.

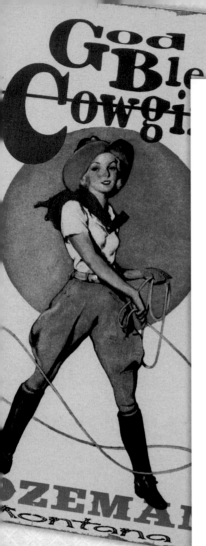

Strange-Sounding Meatballs

They may sound strange, but these unusual meatballs from Elaine Block (Sister #151) are sure to satisfy everyone around the campfire. The sweetness of the sauce provides a nice contrast to the savory meatballs.

Serves 8 to 10

> 2 pounds ground beef
> 1 cup bread crumbs
> 1 package dry onion soup mix
> 3 eggs
> 1 pound sauerkraut (drained)
> 1 bottle chili sauce
> 1 cup water
> 1 cup brown sugar
> 1 cup whole cranberry sauce

Combine the ground beef, bread crumbs, dry onion soup mix, and eggs. Mix well, and form about 25 to 30 golf ball–size meatballs. Place the meatballs in a Dutch oven, and cover evenly with the sauerkraut. In a separate bowl, mix the chili sauce, water, brown sugar, and cranberry sauce. Pour the mixture over the meatballs. Cook over 10 hot briquettes, with 12 briquettes on the lid, for about an hour, until the meat is thoroughly cooked.

Stuffed Bell Peppers

Edith Berry (Sister #614) is acknowledged as one of the best cooks in the Sisterhood. She has collected hundreds of campfire recipes. This old-fashioned favorite can be put together in advance and stored in a cooler until suppertime.

Serves 6

14 soda crackers, crushed into fine pieces
1 1/2 pounds lean ground beef
1 large onion, chopped
3 stalks celery, chopped
1 (14-ounce) can tomato sauce
2 eggs, slightly beaten
2 cloves fresh garlic, minced
6 large red, green, orange, or yellow bell peppers
2 cups water
1/4 cup Parmesan cheese, grated

Start 27 charcoal briquettes. Let them burn until they are covered in light gray ash. In a large bowl, mix together the soda crackers, ground beef, onion, celery, and half the tomato sauce. Add the eggs and garlic and mix well. Cut off the top of the peppers and clean out the insides. Stuff the peppers with the meat mixture and place them in a 14-inch Dutch oven. Add 2 cups water to the bottom of the Dutch oven and steam the peppers for 1 hour, using approximately 12 charcoal briquettes on the bottom of the Dutch oven and 15 on the lid. When the peppers are cooked, pour the remaining tomato sauce over the peppers and sprinkle with Parmesan cheese. Cook for a few more minutes, until the cheese is melted.

Jambalaya

"This hot and spicy Creole dish is always a big hit. Serve with lots of crusty French bread and ice-cold beer." —Edith Berry (Sister #614)

Serves 6 to 8

2 cups reduced-sodium chicken broth
1 1/2 cups V8 juice
2 teaspoons paprika
1 1/2 teaspoons kosher salt
1/4 teaspoon freshly ground black pepper
1 teaspoon Tabasco sauce
2 tablespoons vegetable oil
1 cup chopped yellow onion
1/2 cup chopped red bell pepper
1/2 cup chopped celery
1/2 pound smoked dinner sausage, diced
2 teaspoons minced garlic
1 bay leaf
1 1/2 cups long grain rice
1/2 pound Black Forest ham, diced
1 pound medium shrimp (approximately 35 count),
    peeled and deveined (leave tails on)
2 tablespoons finely chopped Italian parsley

In a small saucepan, combine the chicken broth, V8 juice, paprika, salt, pepper, and Tabasco. Cover and place pan over direct medium heat. When liquid comes to a boil, remove the pan from the heat and set aside.

In a large Dutch oven, heat the oil over approximately 10 briquettes. When the oil is hot, add the onion, bell pepper, and celery. Cook for 3 to 5 minutes, until the vegetables soften, stirring often.

Add the sausage, garlic, and bay leaf and cook for 2 to 3 minutes, stirring often. Stir in the rice and ham. Add the warm chicken broth mixture and stir.

Slide the Dutch oven to the edge of your fire so it will barely simmer; *do not boil.* Cover and let simmer for about 18 minutes, until the rice is cooked through but not mushy, stirring once or twice and making sure there is still some liquid left. If the mixture looks dry, add a little coffee or chicken broth. *Make sure the mixture does not boil.* (If the mixture starts to boil, move some briquettes out from under the Dutch oven.)

Add shrimp and stir to combine. Cover the pot and cook for 3 to 5 minutes, until the shrimp are done but still tender. Remove the Dutch oven from the fire and discard the bay leaf. Season to taste—remember it is *hot, hot, hot!* Add more salt or Tabasco if needed. Let stand with lid on for 5 minutes, then stir in parsley and serve.

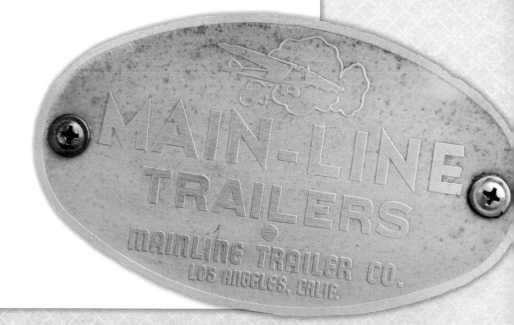

Apricot-Braised Pork Loin

"A more elegant dish than you'd normally see around a campfire, this pork loin features the slightly peppery taste of watercress, which contrasts nicely with the sweetness of the apricot sauce. The dish is particularly good when served with boiled new potatoes." —EDITH BERRY (SISTER #614)

Serves 8

1/8 cup vegetable oil
4 pounds boneless pork loin roast
2 cups chopped onions
2 cups chopped carrots
2 cloves garlic, minced
4 (12-ounce) cans apricot nectar
2 teaspoons dried mustard
2 teaspoons salt
Bunch of watercress, chopped

Start 14 charcoal briquettes. Let them burn until they are covered with light gray ash. Heat the oil in a 12-inch Dutch oven until it reaches about 400°F. Add the pork roast. Brown pork on all sides. After browning, insert a meat thermometer into the thickest part of the meat. Add the onions, carrots, and garlic. Cook approximately 8 to 10 minutes, until onions are tender. Add the apricot nectar, mustard, salt, and enough water to almost cover the pork. Bring to a boil. Cover and bake at about 375°F (take out one or two briquettes, if necessary). The meat is done when the thermometer reads 170°F. Remove pork and keep warm. Boil pan juices for about 5 minutes, until thickened. Serve pork with sauce and garnish with watercress.

Dutch Oven Mac and Cheese

This crowd pleaser from Christa Branch (Sister #883) is easily customized by changing the type of cheese or meat.

Serves 6 to 8

> 12 ounces elbow macaroni
> 12 ounces grated Mexican-blend cheese, plus some extra for the top
> 1/2 pound small cubed ham
> 1/4 cup flour
> 1 cup half-and-half
> Salt and pepper
> Crushed crackers or potato chips

Parboil macaroni. (You can do this at home, and then place the macaroni in a zippy bag and take it with you to your campout in the cooler.) Combine the first six ingredients in a large bowl and fold everything together. Place in an oiled Dutch oven and cover with some extra cheese and crushed crackers or potato chips. Bake for 50 minutes to an hour (until bubbly) with 8 briquettes underneath and 14 to 16 on top, rotating oven every 10 to 15 minutes. Let stand for 10 minutes before serving.

Grandmother's Shepherd's Pie

Cheri McDonald (Sister #802), one of the Dutch Oven Divas, makes this shepherd's pie in her Grandmother's Dutch oven.

Serves 6 to 8

2 pounds ground beef or lamb (Grandmother used lamb)
2 cups chopped carrots
2 cups chopped celery
1 cup chopped onion
2 tablespoons rosemary, plus extra for sprinkling on top
2 tablespoons thyme, plus extra for sprinkling on top
Salt and pepper
2 tablespoons flour
4 to 5 cups mashed potatoes

In a 12-inch Dutch oven, brown the meat, carrots, celery, and onion. Add the rosemary, thyme, salt, and pepper. When the meat is good and browned, add the flour and mix well. Top the meat mixture with mashed potatoes, and sprinkle with a little rosemary and thyme.

Cook in a Dutch oven over 6 to 8 briquettes, with 12 on top. Bake covered for 35 to 45 minutes.

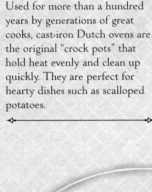

Used for more than a hundred years by generations of great cooks, cast-iron Dutch ovens are the original "crock pots" that hold heat evenly and clean up quickly. They are perfect for hearty dishes such as scalloped potatoes.

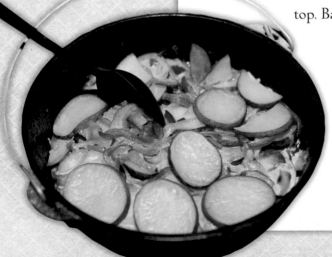

Cheese Grits

These are a favorite with the Southern Sisters and are great as a side with eggs, meat, or fish.

Serves 8

> 6 cups water
> 1 teaspoon salt
> 1 1/2 cups grits
> 1/2 cup butter
> 1 pound cheddar cheese, grated
> 3 eggs, beaten

In a Dutch oven, bring water to a boil and add salt. Stir in the grits and cook for 5 minutes. Add the butter and cheese. Stir and cook for 5 minutes. Add the eggs and stir. Bake over 6 briquettes with 8 on top for 40 minutes.

Cheese Grits

6 cups boiling water
1 1/2 cup grits
1 tsp. salt
1 lb. grated cheddar cheese
3 eggs
1/2 cup. butter
Stir grits into salted boiling water for 5 mins.
Add butter + cheese.
Stir + Cool for 5 mins.
Beat eggs + stir into grits
Bake in Dutch oven 40 mins.

Cow-Chip Biscuits

These basic biscuits are from Arlene Tribble (Sister #12), who says they are called cow-chip biscuits because they were cooked over cow chips by the early settlers of the American West.

Makes approximately 18 biscuits.

> 3 cups flour
> 6 teaspoons baking powder
> 1 teaspoon salt
> 1 tablespoon sugar
> 3 tablespoons shortening
> 1 1/3 cups milk

Sift together all the dry ingredients. Cut in the shortening until flaky pieces form. Add the milk and mix until sticky. Turn onto floured board. Pat gently until dough is about 1/2 inch thick. Cut out biscuits with a biscuit cutter or the floured rim of a water glass. Place biscuits in a large greased, warmed Dutch oven. Do not crowd. Cover and place approximately 20 hot briquettes on the lid. Bake for about 20 minutes. Serve with honey, jam, or chili.

Dutch Oven Dump Cobbler

Don't forget dessert! This simple cobbler from Debbie Veldhuis (Sister #135) is made from a few items picked up at the local grocery store. Serve with vanilla ice cream or whipped cream.

Serves 10 to 12

3 cans of fruit pie filling (your choice)
1 box cake mix (your choice)
Butter or margarine
Brown sugar

Into a well-seasoned 12- or 14-quart Dutch oven, open and dump the contents of the 3 cans of fruit filling. Dump in the cake mix and spread it evenly over the top, but do not stir up the contents. Dot the top with butter. Sprinkle with brown sugar.

Put the lid on the Dutch oven and place it over about 6 briquettes, with 8 briquettes on top. Bake for about 30 to 45 minutes. Rotate the Dutch oven four times during baking. The cobbler is done when the fruit is bubbling through the cake mix and no cake mix powder is visible. Remove Dutch oven from briquettes. The cobbler will continue to bake while the oven cools.

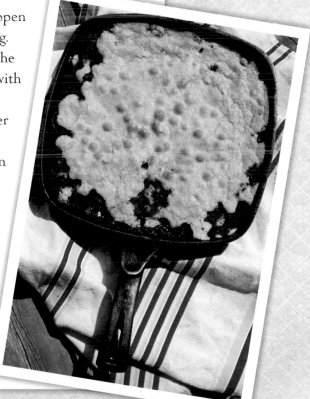

Time for dessert: A fresh blackberry cobbler is served straight from the cast-iron skillet—covered for cooking, uncovered for serving.

Banana Dump Cobbler

This proven campout favorite from Christi Partee (Sister #687) is a sweet and tasty way to use up extra bananas.

Serves 10 to 12

- 1 yellow cake mix, prepared according to package directions
- 5 pounds peeled bananas
- 2 sticks margarine
- 1 pound brown sugar
- 1 tablespoon cinnamon
- 3 tablespoons white sugar

Heat the Dutch oven and cover it with 8 briquettes for 15 minutes. Prepare cake mix and set aside. Slice bananas lengthwise and set aside. Remove preheated oven from briquettes and melt the butter in the bottom. Add the brown sugar and mix well. Add the bananas and sauté for 3 minutes over fire. Pour the cake mixture over the bananas.

Fold the banana mixture up over the cake mixture a few times. Sprinkle with the cinnamon and white sugar. Bake for 35 minutes. Rotate the Dutch oven four times during baking. For the first 10 minutes, use 8 briquettes on the bottom only. Then add 8 briquettes to the top and continue baking until the cake tests done.

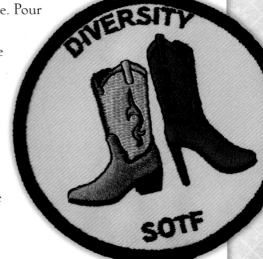

Dutch Oven Apple Crisp

Everyone loves apple desserts, but how often do we have the time to bake? This dessert from Julianne Campbell (Sister #1075) is easy to make and a real favorite.

Serves 10 to 12

> 10 to 15 good-sized Granny Smith or other tart apples
> 1 cup of brown sugar, firmly packed
> 1 box yellow cake mix
> 1 stick butter, unsalted
> Cinnamon

Start the charcoal (approximately 25 briquettes) with a chimney or a large camp burner. Core and slice the apples into about 6 slices per apple. Line the Dutch oven with heavy-duty aluminum foil (for easy cleanup). Place apples in the bottom of the oven. Sprinkle brown sugar on top, and then cover with the cake mix. Do not stir. Cut up the stick of butter and place pats on top of the cake mix. Sprinkle with a little cinnamon. Place about 10 charcoal briquettes underneath the oven and 10 to 15 on top. Cook for 45 minutes to an hour. Rotate the Dutch oven four times during baking. Check after 30 to 35 minutes. It is done when the crust starts to brown and you can see the apple mixture bubbling up through the crust.

Award-Winning Chili

No camp cookout is complete without chili! Becky Clarke (Sister #2), Vickie Stoppello (Sister #5), and Ferne Krumm (Sister #28) developed this recipe, which won the McCall, Idaho, chili cook-off in 2009. Serve with a fresh green salad and cornbread for a delicious and filling meal.

Serves 8 to 10

4 pounds beef chuck, trimmed and cut into 1/2-inch cubes
Kosher salt and fresh ground pepper
4 tablespoons canola oil
4 medium yellow onions, chopped
4 cloves garlic, finely chopped
2 (6-ounce) cans tomato paste
4 tablespoons dried oregano
3 tablespoons New Mexico chili powder
4 teaspoons cayenne pepper
1 tablespoon sweet paprika
1 teaspoon ground cumin
1 tablespoon Tabasco sauce
4 to 5 cups of water
1/2 cup lime juice
1 can lager beer

OPPOSITE: Emily Schreiner (Sister #968) prepares her contribution to the evening's meal from the back of her teardrop trailer.

Season the beef with salt and pepper. Heat the oil in a 6-quart pot over high heat and brown the meat in 3 or 4 batches. Add the onions and garlic and cook until lightly browned; return the beef to the pot and add the tomato paste. Cook about 12 minutes, stirring with a wooden spoon. Add the spices and Tabasco sauce and cook for 1 minute. Add 4 cups water and simmer for 2 hours, stirring occasionally, until meat is tender. If the chili becomes too thick, add 1 cup water. Add the lime juice and beer, and cook about 1 more hour; taste for seasoning.

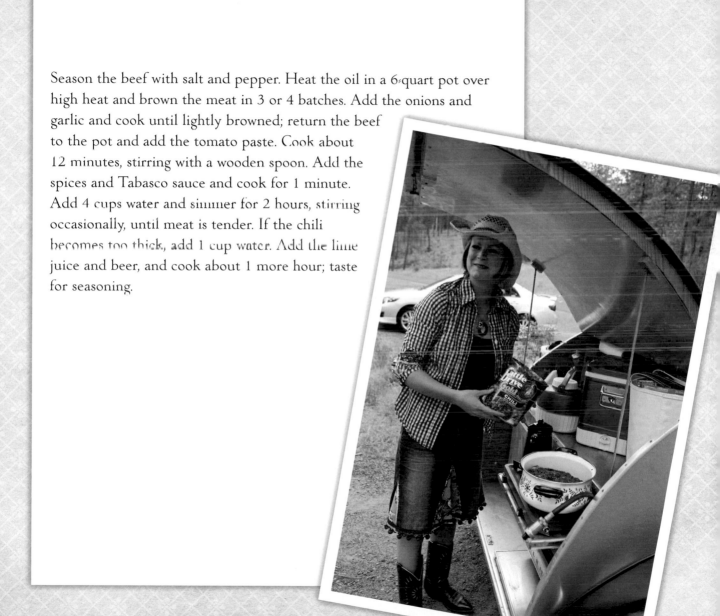

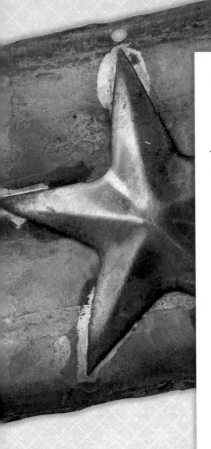

Bread on a Stick

If you're feeling lazy, bring along some canned biscuit dough, crack open the can, flatten the biscuits with your hands, and wrap them around a stick.

Serves 12

> 3 cups flour
> Pinch of salt
> 1 teaspoon baking powder
> 2 tablespoons lard or Crisco (canola or corn oil can be used as a substitute)
> Water
> Butter
> Cinnamon
> Sugar

Before leaving on your trip, mix the dry ingredients and the lard in a large sealable container. Just before cooking, gradually add the water to the dry ingredients. Mix with your hands or a stick. Your dough should be slightly sticky, so it will adhere to itself and the stick. Don't add too much water or your dough will be too runny.

Take some dough and wrap it around a stick. Cook it over the campfire. When your bread on a stick is nicely browned, remove it from the stick. If it slides off easily, it's ready. If it clings to the stick, it needs to cook longer.

Spread it with butter, sprinkle with cinnamon and sugar, and enjoy.

About the Stick

Select a piece of straight, dry, wood, about the thickness of your thumb and about as long as an adult's arm. Using a sharp knife, shave the bark off one end of the stick. The stick does not need to be pointed. Tip: Don't use green wood. It will give your bread on a stick a bitter taste.

Eggs Hopeful

Rebecca Price (Sister #274) calls this the ultimate comfort food. The recipe comes from her dad, who would fix this in hunting camp before he and his friends headed out in the "hopes" of bagging a deer.

Serves 4 to 6

2 medium onions, chopped
1 green pepper, chopped
2 tablespoons butter or olive oil
1 (28-ounce) can of tomatoes, chopped
6 slices of bread, crumbled
1 teaspoon dry oregano
1 teaspoon dry basil
1 tablespoon chili powder
1 teaspoon Worcestershire sauce
1/2 cup grated Parmesan cheese
2 cloves garlic, crushed
8 eggs (or at least 2 eggs/person)

In a large skillet, sauté the onions and pepper in butter until soft. Add the tomatoes, bread, oregano, basil, chili powder, and Worcestershire sauce. With a large spoon, smash up the tomatoes and stir until the mixture is pretty uniform in texture. Simmer until thickened. Stir in the cheese and garlic. When the cheese is melted, use the bowl of the spoon to create indentations in the mix. Break an egg in each indentation. Cover with a lid and cook until the eggs firm up.

Molly's Favorite Chili

After a day of fresh air, sunshine, and outdoor activities, you want a hearty meal that can be thrown together in a matter of moments. Here it is—from Molly Westgate (Sister #190). It's even better the next day.

Serves 8

- 1 pound ground turkey
- 1 pound ground beef
- 1 medium onion, chopped
- 2 (14-ounce) cans beans (your choice—kidney, pinto, etc.)
- 2 (14-ounce) cans chopped or crushed tomatoes
- 1 (8-ounce) can tomato sauce
- 3 to 4 tablespoons chili powder
- 1 teaspoon ground cumin
- 1 teaspoon salt
- 1 teaspoon pepper
- 1/2 cup chopped green peppers (optional)
- 1 (8-ounce) can diced mild chilies (optional)

Brown the meat. Add the onions halfway through. Cook until the onions are soft, and then drain. Add the rest of the ingredients; cook for 20 minutes.

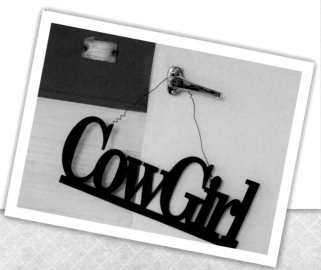

Green Chile Stew

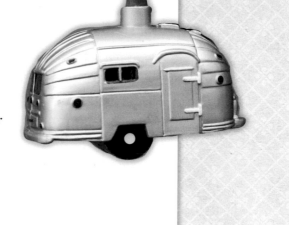

This versatile stew from Diane Smith (Sister #16) also makes a delicious sauce for smothered burritos or breakfast casseroles. Add a few teaspoons of corn starch (mixed with 1/4 cup cold water) at the end for a thicker stew.

Serves 6 to 8

> 2 pounds lean pork, chicken, or beef, cubed
> 3 tablespoons vegetable oil
> 1 large onion, chopped
> 2 cloves garlic, chopped
> 6 to 10 green chilies, roasted, peeled, seeds and stems removed, chopped or one
>   (14-ounce) can chilies, drained
> 1 large potato, peeled and diced
> 2 or 3 tomatoes, peeled and chopped
> 1 (10-ounce) can diced tomatoes with green chilies
> 3 cups water
> 1/2 teaspoon cumin
> Salt and pepper

Brown the meat in hot oil. Add the onion and garlic and sauté for a few minutes. Add everything else. Cover and simmer for about 2 hours, until the meat is very tender. Serve with warm tortillas.

Fennel and Chimichurri Salad

MaryJane Butters (Sister #1315) celebrates the everyday organic lifestyle on her farm and in her garden. She writes about it in her magazine, MaryJanesFarm.

Serves 6 to 8

10 large russet potatoes
Olive oil
Salt and pepper
1/3 cup Chimichurri Sauce (recipe below)
1 bulb fennel, thinly sliced

CHIMICHURRI SAUCE

Makes 1 1/2 cups

1/4 cup finely chopped onion
1/2 cup parsley, finely chopped
3 tablespoons cilantro, finely chopped
3 cloves garlic, minced
1/2 teaspoon salt
1/2 teaspoon cumin
1/2 teaspoon crushed red pepper
1/4 teaspoon freshly ground black pepper
1/2 cup olive oil
1/4 cup red wine vinegar

Mix all the ingredients and let stand at room temperature for 2 hours.

Bake the potatoes ahead of time as you normally would, but remove them from the oven the minute they are done. Overbaking will make them difficult to skewer. You want them slightly al dente. Cut the potatoes, skins and all, into 3/4-inch cubes and then skewer them. Brush the potatoes generously with the olive oil, and sprinkle with salt and pepper. Place skewers on a campfire grill top and cook, turning frequently, until golden brown and crispy. Remove from the fire and toss with the Chimichurri Sauce and fennel while still warm. Serve immediately.

MaryJane Butters (Sister #1315) makes this chimichurri potato salad (delicately flavored with fennel) in the back of her custom teardrop.

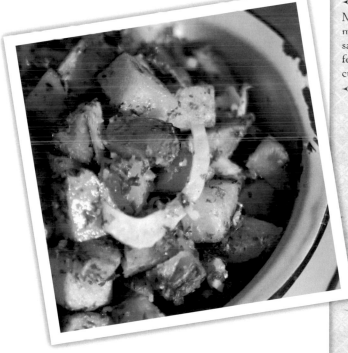

Turkey in a Trash Can

Sound scary? This method from Glenda (G!) Stone (Sister #62) is actually a simple and efficient way to roast a turkey in the great outdoors. Use your favorite spices to amp up the flavor and serve with roasted or steamed veggies.

Serves 12 to 15

1 (20-pound) turkey
Salt and pepper
Garlic powder
Roll of heavy-duty aluminum foil
10 pounds of sand (if your campsite is in a rocky area)
18- to 20-inch wooden 2 × 2
20-gallon metal trash can, clean
30 pounds of charcoal
Small camp shovel
Thermal gloves

Wash the turkey, remove the neck and giblets, and season with salt, pepper, and garlic powder. Set aside. Line a 4-foot-square area on the ground with aluminum foil. If the surface is rocky, you will need to put sand under the foil to even it out. In the middle of the foil, drive the 2 × 2 into the ground, leaving enough height for the bird to "sit" on it. Cover the 2 × 2 with heavy-duty foil.

Place the turkey on the 2 × 2. Turn the trash can upside down, centering it on the turkey. Twist the can a little to make a good seal in the sand to trap the heat inside. Put as much charcoal as you can on top of the trash can. Mound the remainder of the 30 pounds around the trash can. Light the charcoal. After the charcoal is hot (about 30 minutes) start timing the turkey. Let it cook for about 1 1/2 hours. Use a shovel to remove the briquettes from around the trash can. Use gloves to remove the can. Use the trash can lid as a serving platter.

Dolly V's Riverside Salmon

Salmon doesn't get any easier than this. Kristin Manas (Sister #29) suggests filling a second foil packet with potatoes or vegetables, throwing it on the fire with the fish, and enjoying a lovely riverside meal.

Serves 4 to 6

    2 sticks butter
    2/3 cups brown sugar, firmly packed
    Juice of one lemon
    1/4 cup soy sauce
    1 1/2 pounds salmon filet
    Lemon wedges

Place the butter, brown sugar, lemon juice, and soy sauce in a saucepan. Heat until the sugar is dissolved. Place the salmon on a large piece of heavy-duty aluminum foil and cover it with sauce. Seal the foil and cook on hot briquettes for approximately 20 minutes or until the fish flakes with a fork. Serve with lemon wedges.

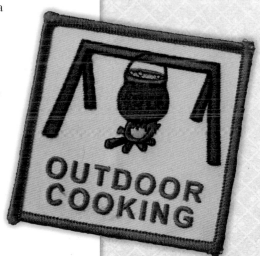

PawPaw's Sweet Beans

Nina Elliott (Sister #231) says her dad (PawPaw) made these beans at family barbecues and campouts. They were a big hit with young and old.

Serves 4

> 2 slices bacon, diced
> 1/2 small onion, diced
> 1 (15-ounce) can of pork and beans
> 1/2 cup brown sugar, loosely packed
> 1 teaspoon Worcestershire sauce

In a saucepan, cook the bacon over medium heat for a few minutes, then add the onion. Stir occasionally and cook until both start to brown. Add the pork and beans, brown sugar, and Worcestershire sauce. Simmer on low heat for about 10 minutes to allow flavors to blend.

Southern Sisters make sure that there is plenty of everyone's favorite beverage to go around, and they serve it in canning jars.

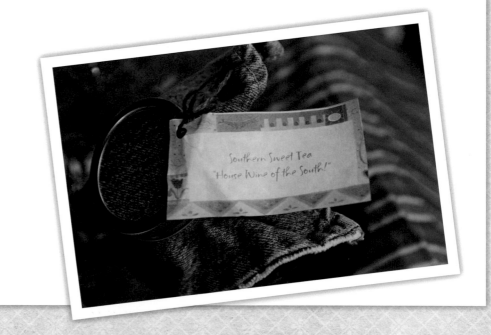

Tacky Trailer Campfire Trout

Not as tacky as it sounds, this quick and simple recipe from Kristin Manas (Sister #29) brings out the flavor of your fresh catch.

Serves 4 to 6

> 1 whole trout
> 1 small onion, sliced
> 1 small lemon, sliced
> 2 tablespoons butter
> Salt and pepper

Put the trout on a large piece of heavy-duty aluminum foil. Top with the sliced onion, lemon slices, butter, salt, and pepper. Seal the foil, making slits for steam to escape. Cook on briquettes for 30 minutes or until the fish flakes with a fork.

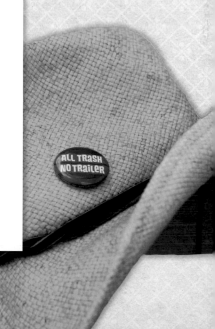

Fry Bread

Maurrie Sussman (Sister #1) got this recipe from Annie Bedonie, a Navajo woman known for her fabulous fry bread, during one of the Sisters' annual trips to fish on Navajo lands.

Makes about 12 fry breads

> 5 cups flour
> 1 teaspoon baking powder
> 1/2 teaspoon salt
> 1 teaspoon shortening
> 3 cups warm water
> Vegetable oil

In a large mixing bowl, mix the flour, baking powder, salt, and shortening. Add the water slowly, mixing with your hands. (Use your hands, not a spoon, because you need to feel it.) Knead the dough until it no longer feels sticky. Cover it with a towel and let it sit for 5 minutes.

In a frying pan, add enough vegetable oil to reach your first knuckle. Heat the oil until it bubbles. Take a hunk of dough the size of a golf ball and work it in your hands—stretching and clapping with it—until it reaches the size of a salad plate. It will be thick. Place the dough in hot oil and fry 2 to 3 minutes, until it turns golden brown. Turn and brown the other side. Remove it from the pan, and drain it on paper towels. Serve hot with butter and honey.

Berry Dessert

Fresh berries from the local farmers' market quickly become a sweet treat with the addition of just a few other ingredients and a short time on the briquettes. This has been a Sisters favorite for so long, no one remembers where the recipe came from.

Serves 8

> 1 stick butter, melted
> 1 cup sugar
> 1 cup flour
> 2 eggs, beaten
> 1 cup fresh berries (any kind will do)

Start the charcoal briquettes and let them burn until they are covered with light gray ash, about 30 minutes. Combine the butter, sugar, flour, and eggs. Mix well. Spread the berries evenly over the bottom of a greased 9-inch iron skillet with a lid. Pour the batter over the fruit. Cover the skillet and place it on the hot briquettes. Heap more hot briquettes on the lid. Bake for 40 minutes or until brown and bubbly. Serve immediately

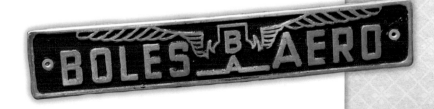

Sisters on the Fly Soft Granola Bars

These scrumptious bars are the perfect make-ahead, take-along snack. Anita Wallace (Sister #440) says these bars will keep for up to two weeks in a tightly covered container, but she admits they won't last that long.

Makes approximately 28 two-inch bars.

1 cup brown sugar, firmly packed
1 cup vegetable oil
2 eggs
2 cup oats (regular or quick)
1 1/2 cups flour
1 cup raisins, chopped dates, or dried cherries
1 cup chopped nuts (your choice)
1 cup flaked coconut
1 teaspoon baking soda
1/4 teaspoon salt
1 1/2 teaspoons ground cinnamon
1 1/2 teaspoons ground allspice
Pinch of ground cloves

HONEY GLAZE
1/4 cup honey
2 tablespoon butter

Heat honey and butter in a small pan, stirring until melted and hot.

Preheat the oven to 350°F. Grease a 15 1/2 × 10 1/2-inch jelly roll pan. Mix the sugar, oil, and eggs in a large bowl with a spoon until smooth. Stir in the remaining ingredients. Spread the mixture in the jelly roll pan, patting evenly by hand. Bake for 17 to 22 minutes, until the center is set but not firm. Drizzle with Honey Glaze. Cool completely. Cut into bars.

Never Fail Banana Bread

Perfect for a quick breakfast or an early afternoon snack, this recipe from Molly Westgate (Sister #190) makes two regular loaves but can be halved to make one loaf.

2 sticks margarine or butter
2 cups sugar
6 ripe bananas, mashed
4 eggs
4 cups flour
2 teaspoons salt
2 teaspoons baking soda
1/2 cup chopped nuts
1 teaspoon vanilla

Preheat the oven to 350°F. Cream the butter and sugar. Add the ripe bananas and mix well. Add the eggs and then the dry ingredients, and mix. Add the nuts and vanilla at the end.

Divide into two loaf pans. Bake for 1 hour, until a toothpick comes out dry

Ahhh . . . Happy Camper wine and a platter of fresh fruit. These ladies know how to live.

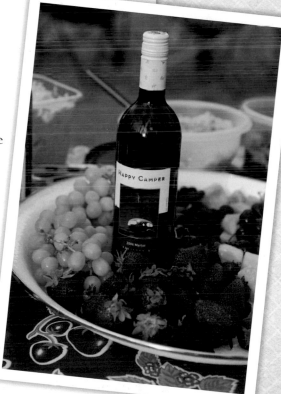

Bread Pudding

This simple rendition of a classic dessert from Chris Kirk (Sister #3) will satisfy everyone's sweet tooth with minimal work.

Serves 6 to 8

2 cups milk
1/2 cup butter
1 teaspoon vanilla
2 eggs, beaten
4 cups cubed bread
1/2 cup chocolate chips

Combine the milk and butter in a saucepan and cook over low heat until butter is melted. Add the vanilla. Remove from heat and let cool. Preheat oven to 350°F. In a large bowl, combine the eggs and milk mixture and stir, and then add the bread, stirring only minimally. Add the chocolate chips, stirring as little as possible. Transfer to a greased 9 × 9-inch baking dish, and bake for 50 minutes, until set.

Lemon Curd

This lemon curd from Elaine Block (Sister #151) is best enjoyed when spooned over raisin bread, pudding, or scones.

Makes approximately 2 cups

> 6 tablespoons unsalted butter, softened
> 1 cup sugar
> 2 large eggs, plus 2 large egg yolks
> 2/3 cup fresh lemon juice
> 1 teaspoon grated lemon zest

In a large bowl, beat the butter and sugar with a mixer for about 2 minutes. Slowly add the eggs and yolks. Beat for 1 minute. Mix in the lemon juice. The mixture will look curdled, but will smooth out as it cooks. In a medium heavy-based saucepan, cook the mixture over low heat until it looks smooth. (The curdled look goes away as the butter in the mixture melts.)

Increase the heat to medium and cook, stirring constantly, until the mixture thickens, about 15 minutes. It should leave a path on the back of a spoon, and it will read 170°F on a candy thermometer. Don't let the mixture boil. Remove from the heat and stir in the zest. Transfer to a bowl. Press plastic wrap on the surface to keep a skin from forming and chill in the refrigerator. It will thicken more as it cools. Cover tightly; it will keep in the refrigerator for a week and in the freezer for 2 months.

Devonshire Cream

Elaine Block (Sister #151) is the dessert-sauce queen. The Sisters love, love, love her make-ahead, take-along sauces that fancy up everything from bread to scones.

Makes approximately 5 cups

> 1 cup cool water
> 1 package gelatin powder
> 2 cups heavy cream
> 2 teaspoons vanilla
> 1/2 cup sugar
> 2 cups (16 ounces) sour cream

Pour the water into a mixing bowl. Sprinkle the gelatin on top, and place it in the freezer for 10 minutes. Remove it from the freezer and heat it in a microwave for 1 minute. Set aside to cool. In the meantime, whip the heavy cream, vanilla, and sugar in a medium bowl until stiff. Once the water mixture is cool, mix in the sour cream with a rubber spatula. Fold in the whipped cream. Store in two preserve jars in the refrigerator for up to 1 week.

Hot Fudge Sauce

Why settle for store-bought when you can make a homemade sauce from Elaine Block (Sister #151) in just a few minutes? Drizzle this hot fudge sauce over ice cream, bread pudding, or just about anything.

Makes approximately 2 cups

> 4 (1-ounce) squares semisweet chocolate (or 3/4 cup semisweet chocolate chips)
> 2 tablespoons butter
> 1 (14-ounce) can sweetened condensed milk
> 1 teaspoon vanilla
> Dash salt
> 2 to 3 tablespoons Amaretto or your choice of liquor (optional)

In a heavy saucepan over low heat, melt the chocolate and butter; add the milk, vanilla, and salt. Cook, stirring constantly, for about 5 minutes or until the sauce is thickened. Remove from heat and add Amaretto. Refrigerate. Keeps for 2 weeks.

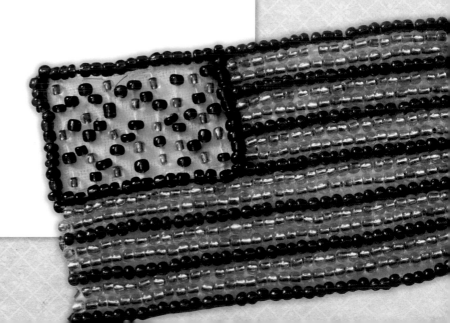

Tequila Gazpacho Salad

From Teri Lowrie (Sister #48), this cool and refreshing salad is the perfect antidote to a long, hot summer day.

Serves 4

1 cucumber, diced
1 green bell pepper, diced
1 red bell pepper, diced
3 tomatoes, cored and diced
1/2 cup diced red onion
2 cloves garlic, minced
1/4 cup red wine vinegar
2 tablespoons olive oil
1/4 teaspoon salt
1/4 teaspoon cumin
1/4 teaspoon freshly ground black pepper
1 shot of your favorite tequila
1 large avocado

In a large bowl, combine the cucumber, bell peppers, tomatoes, onion, and garlic. In a smaller bowl, whisk together the vinegar, olive oil, salt, cumin, pepper, and tequila. Pour the vinegar mix over the vegetables and refrigerate overnight, stirring occasionally. Just before serving, dice and stir in the avocado.

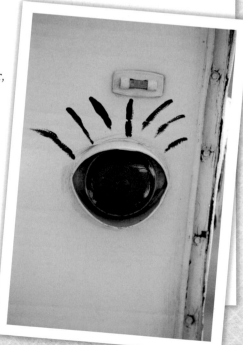

Mississippi Mud Pie

This pie is easy to assemble at the campsite. Debra Bolnick (Sister #45) suggests making the crust ahead of time and bringing the rest of the ingredients with you.

Serves 8

MAKE-AHEAD CRUST
- 1 cup flour
- 1/2 cup butter or margarine, softened
- 1 cup chopped nuts

Preheat the oven to 350°F. Combine the flour, butter, and nuts. Line the bottom of a greased 9 x 13-inch baking pan with the mixture. Bake for 20 minutes. Cool completely.

- 1 cup powdered sugar
- 1 (8-ounce) package cream cheese
- 2 cups Cool Whip
- 1 package chocolate instant pudding
- 3 cups cold milk
- 2 chocolate candy bars, grated
- Chopped pecans

Mix the sugar, cream cheese, and 1 cup of the Cool Whip together and spread over the crust. In a separate bowl, mix the pudding and the milk together until thickened. Spread over cream cheese mixture. Top with the remaining Cool Whip. Garnish with grated chocolate and chopped pecans. Chill in a camp cooler overnight, over ice.

Lemon-Drop Martinis

Becky Clarke (Sister #2), is famous for her elegant lemon-drop martinis, served with powdered sugar on the rim of each glass. "It makes life on the trail just that much more civilized." Becky suggests making the simple syrup in your home kitchen and putting it into a canning jar for use on the trail.

Serves 16 to 20

> **2 cups of Citron Vodka**
> **1 cup lemon juice**
> **1 cup Triple Sec**
> **1/2 cup Simple Syrup**

SIMPLE SYRUP

Makes 1 cup.

> **1 cup water**
> **2 cups sugar**

Bring the water to a boil. Dissolve the sugar into the boiling water. Remove the pan from the heat. Let it cool.

Mix all the ingredients together in a pitcher half-filled with ice. Stir well. Pour the mixture into sugar-rimmed martini glasses and garnish with a twisted peel of lemon.

A batch of Becky Clarke's infamous lemon-drop martinis or some simple lemonade, mixed up in a vintage pitcher, refreshes on a warm summer day.

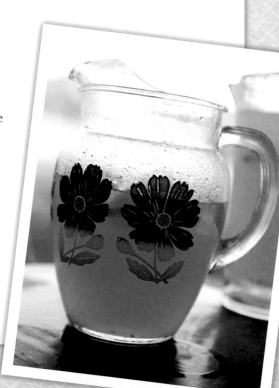

Kudzu Tea

The Southern Sisters know that the fast-growing and invasive ground cover known as kudzu has already taken over the family farm and is about to take over the world. What to do? Pick the smallest, most tender leaves and make tea. L. C. Moon, a naturalist, herbalist, and co-owner (along with her husband, chef Benjamin Keener) of the Wildflower Café in Mentone, Alabama, shares her recipe for kudzu tea.

First make sure the picking area has not been sprayed with chemicals to kill the kudzu. Chop one cup of fresh kudzu leaves and simmer in a quart of water for 30 minutes. Strain and serve (iced or hot) with honey and a sprig of fresh mint.

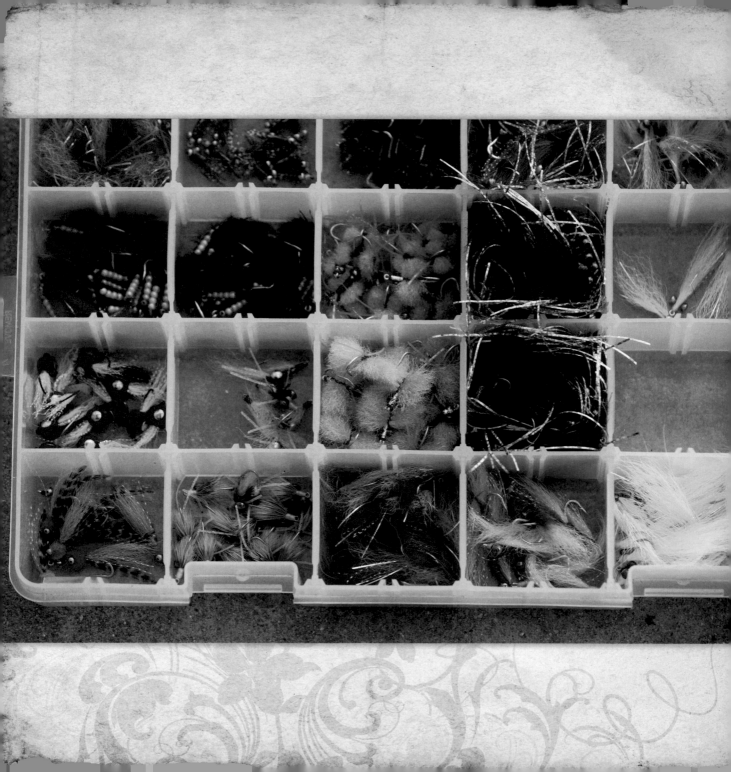

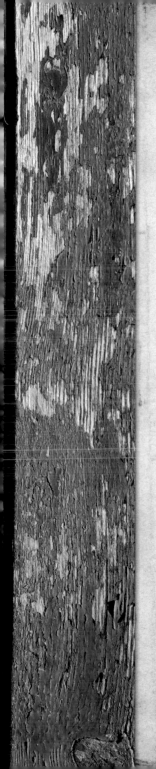

NINE

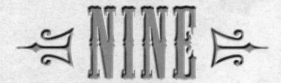

FISH STORIES

For some people, fly-fishing is about catching fish. For others, it is about being out in nature with a stated goal—catching fish—but not worrying whether that goal is met or not. The fishing Sisters are pretty equally divided on this.

Some of the best fishing happens at twilight when the quiet of darkness is fast approaching; when the reds, yellows, and oranges of the sunset's afterglow are playing across the western horizon and creating quick sparks in a fast-moving stream. The nighthawks are dipping and diving over the water after the hatch of insects just emerging. Maybe mayflies, maybe caddis flies. The trout know there's a hatch, too, and they are hungry, which makes for successful fishing. You choose your fly carefully, trying to match the hatch in size and shape. The trout are not easily fooled. They can tell—all too often—a real bug from a fake.

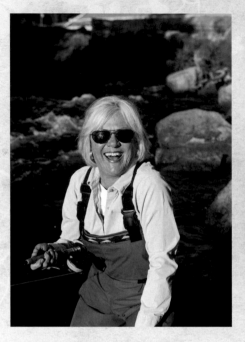

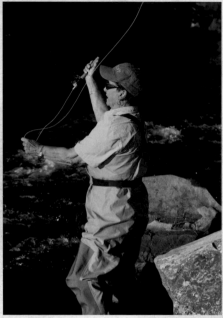

As you stand waist-deep in the river, there is no wind to carry your line astray; only the rush of the water as it presses against you and heads downstream. You listen. You watch. You breathe in deeply and exhale. The rhythm of the cast, the upstream "mend" of the line, the act of stripping the line back and casting again is soothing, even spiritual. Casting is the dance; the catch is a nod to your luck or prowess. But all the while, you know that it's not really about the fishing. It is about sharing this magical time and space with all the beauty of the nature around you—the mountains, the meadows, the fast-rushing stream, the fading light of a perfect evening.

There's no doubt that some Sisters fish to catch a delicious supper, but most enjoy fly-fishing because of the opportunity it provides to get in touch with a simpler self, a simpler time, a simpler life.

WHAT'S SO COOL ABOUT FLY-FISHING?

Fishing is a sport. It is a great way to get exercise while being outdoors on a fine day. Some of the Sisters were fishers before they joined; others joined to learn how to fish. Others never fish at all. But they all enjoy the way the sun dances on the water, sprinkling it with pixie dust and making it gleam like tiny diamonds caught in the light—there for a moment, then gone. A rushing stream carries with it a certain romance. Standing there, you feel the warmth of the day on your skin and a melodious breeze (yes, it does sing a little) blowing through your hair with a sweetness that's difficult to describe but, once experienced, impossible to forget.

As you sit quietly on a rock—beside a stream or right in the middle of it—you start to notice things. The spicy scent of the pine forest. Small creatures that scamper about seemingly in random play.

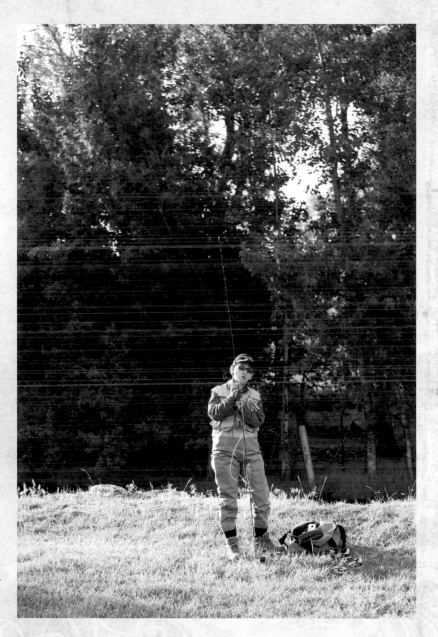

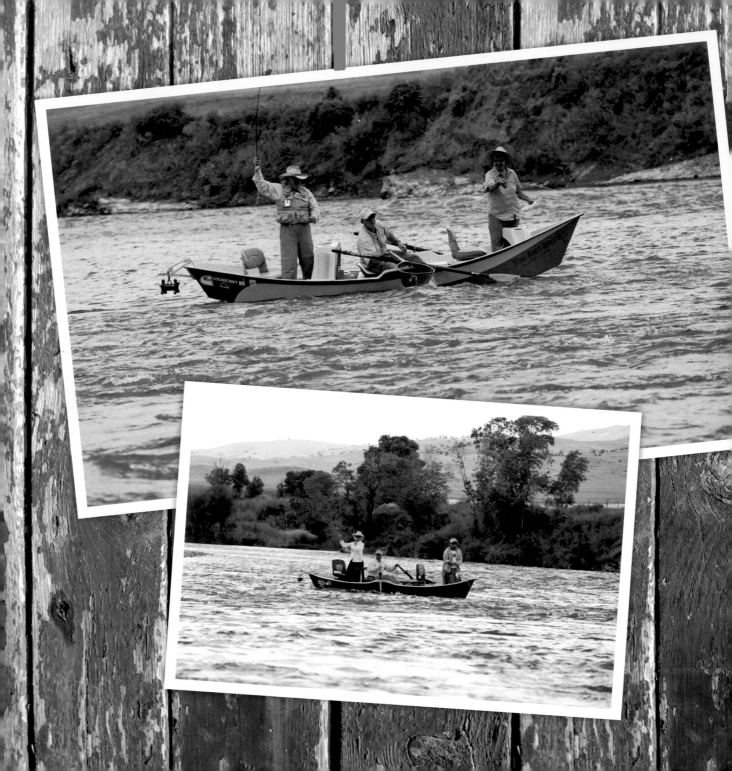

The perfect pitch of a songbird. The creek flows through willows where deer might bed for the night. Fish dart about in the shallows; birds swoop and call from their perches in the pines. Rocky outcroppings define the rugged terrain, their perimeters bordered with the blue-gray colors of sage and the tawny dry grasses.

In the East, streams are ringed with sweet grass and have a mossy overhang reminiscent of *Wind in the Willows*. The sky is a color you will never find in your crayon box; it is so pure, so blue, that it simply cannot be re-created. The quietness hums in your ears and feels like it could swallow up the day with its peaceful charm; there's just a tiny breeze but not a sound of humanity—only nature in its everyday routine.

After a while, human nature being what it is, you will want to do something. Skip a stone across the stream? Maybe. But more likely, you'll want to drop a line into the stream to see if something is attracted to it—and to you. Before long, you'll be trying to think like a fish and throwing only what you imagine that big trout might want to eat. That's how fly-fishing starts for many Sisters, and that's how it grows into a lifelong passion.

FISHING WITH MAZIE

Maurrie and Becky (Sisters #1 and #2) like to catch fish. "Mazie started us out fishing when we were babies," says Maurrie. "We lived in different places (Dad was in the Marine Corps and often on deployment) but always near water, and we fished off the dock. Worms were just fine."

Austin Lowder (Maurrie's son and Mazie's grandson) fished every day from the time he was a child. After college, he moved to Montana to be a fishing guide on the Gallatin River.

"That's where I learned to fly-fish—from my son on the Gallatin River," says Maurrie. "You know that's where *A River Runs Through It* was

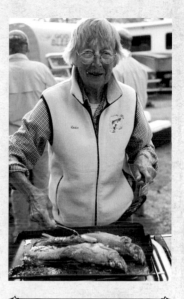

OPPOSITE TOP: The fly-fishing skill of Kathy Wolfe (Sister #10) pays off. She lands the big one while drift boating down the deepest part of the Yellowstone River.

OPPOSITE BOTTOM: Whether in a boat with a guide or alone on the water's edge, most of the Sisters are strictly catch-and-release fishers.

ABOVE: The Sisters get to enjoy the fresh catch of the day, prepared simply by Mazie (Sister #4) on a camp stove.

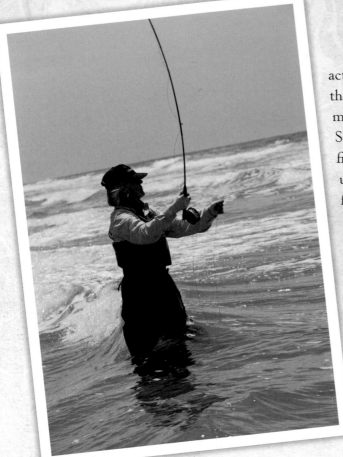

actually filmed." From her son, she also learned the joy of catch and release. Photos and great memories are frequently the only things the Sisters bring home from fly-fishing trips. The fish often stay right where they are. The Sisters use barbless hooks to make catch-and-release fishing easier.

"We keep the fish now and then, but only if we're going to eat it right away," says Maurrie. If that's the plan, they just find a little foil, light a little fire, steam the little fish, and eat it right there on the riverbank. She never keeps the big ones or the fish that fight really hard: "That would be like killing your tennis partner," she says.

Becky agrees. "It is just nice to be able to catch them, give them a little air-kiss, and gently put them back, saying, 'See you again next year.'"

ABOVE: Maurrie Sussman (Sister #1) concentrates on her casting, but actually catching a fish doesn't seem that important when you're surrounded by majestic mountains and standing in a big, blue ocean.

OPPOSITE: Rivers aren't the only place to fly-fish. Kristin Manas (Sister #29) joins the Sisters fly-fishing in the surf at the edge of the Pacific Ocean.

Mazie will tell you that one of the perks of being ninety is that she doesn't get any argument when she says she'd like to keep some fish for dinner. Her recipe for cooking fish is simple—a little olive oil or butter in a skillet ("Cast iron is great but I'm not picky," she says), some flour or cornmeal to roll the fish in, some salt and pepper. While the fish cooks, go make some salad. When the fish's eyes turn white, you know it is done.

The point these Sisters make about keeping a single fish is the same point Sisters make all over the country: Catching a fish is like finding a treasure you've been hunting and working for all day. You don't just help yourself to anything you want; you have to earn the moment when, after a full day of fishing, you cook a fish, sit down with a glass of wine, and eat the fish right out of the frying pan.

"There can't be a better moment than that," says Maurrie, "but you can't do those moments all of the time or they will lose their magic."

Mazie adds, "I don't know if fish can hear things, but if you say, 'The next one's dinner,' you won't catch another fish all day."

A TYPICAL DAY ON THE WATER

First off, there is no such thing as a typical day on a fishing stream. One day the sun is shining. The next day it's raining and the wind is howling. It is difficult to cast into the wind without catching your hook in your hair, in your cap, or on the tip your ear (Ouch! Good thing they're barbless)

But, usually, the Sisters wake up about 6 a.m., drink strong, hot coffee, and meet with their river guide. The guide gives a little talk about where and how long they'll fish, and what they'll catch. If it's a long way to the river, they may decide to take a few of their trailers down to the put-in spot so anyone who wants to take a midday nap can do so. Most often, especially if it is bluebird weather, they'll decide to fish all day with a break for a picnic lunch streamside.

The boats push off from the shore, each carrying two sisters and a guide, who rows the boat across the river in a zigzag pattern, stopping at all the deep holes where the fish like to linger. This is

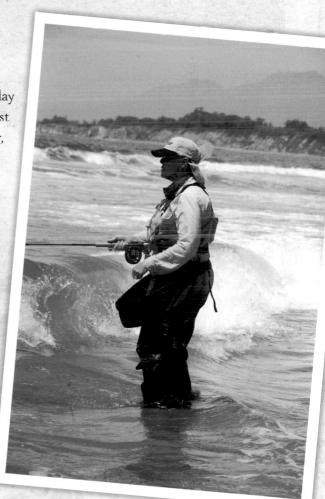

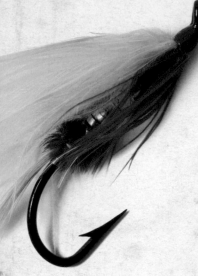

called "useful local knowledge" and is the main reason for hiring a guide. The other reason is that a guide comes to you with a boat.

On a good day, a Sister may catch and release more than twenty fish. On a bad day, none. Whether the fishing is good or stinky, any day is a good day to be with Sisters on the Fly. And everyone looks forward to the fun of après fishing—food, wine, stories around the campfire, and a good night's sleep in your cozy trailer.

FISHING IN SKIRTS . . .

The first book ever published on fly-fishing was written by a woman, Dame Juliana Berners, who published *A Treatyse of Fysshynge wyth an Angle* in 1496. She was a noblewoman and a nun who almost certainly tied her own artificial flies and absolutely certainly fished in a skirt

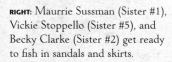

RIGHT: Maurrie Sussman (Sister #1), Vickie Stoppello (Sister #5), and Becky Clarke (Sister #2) get ready to fish in sandals and skirts.

OPPOSITE: Kathy Wolfe (Sister #10), an accomplished fly fisher, watches her fly drift on the calm waters of the Yellowstone River, hoping it will attract a big brown trout.

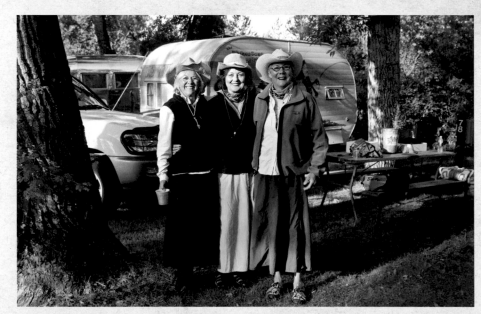

(maybe even her nun's habit). Today, well over a million women fly-fish. Manufacturers have recognized this fact and are making waders that are actually designed for women—rather than women having to buy the closest men's size. Still . . . there is a certain allure to fishing in a skirt.

Ferne Krumm (Sister #28) has a mural painted on the side of her trailer of a willowy Victorian fisherwoman wearing a flowing purple skirt. Ferne calls the woman Syringa, the Latin name for lilacs. "I found her in a thrift store . . . on one of those photo postcards from the late nineteenth century and rescued her and now have her on my trailer," says Ferne, who enjoys fishing in a skirt.

"My first time fishing in a skirt was on the Rock Creek in Red Lodge, Montana. The river comes out of the Bear Tooth Mountains, and I thought I'd be really cold," says Maurrie. With her sandals on and a special quick-drying fishing skirt reaching down to her ankles, she

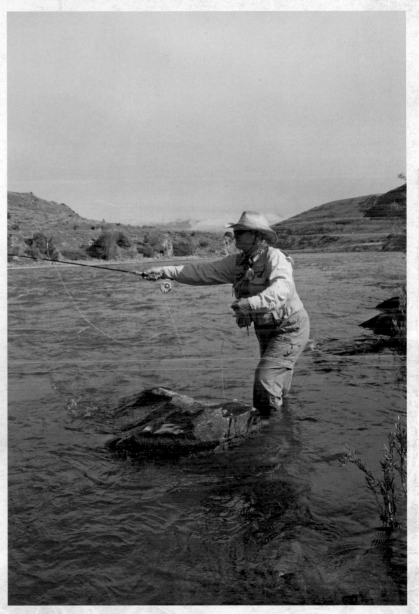

was not cold; she was thrilled. She remembers the skirt getting wet and floating gently on the water. "When you cast the fly line, it is like a ballet with the skirt dancing around your ankles," she says.

Becky, too, loves the freedom of fishing in a skirt. "When your skirt is swishing around your ankles and you're not encumbered by anything, it makes you feel real girly," she says. Something old is new again.

. . . AND OTHER STORIES

It takes a special kind of Sister to go steelhead fishing in February on the Salmon River in the River of No Return Wilderness Area in central Idaho. Accessible only on horseback or by boat, this is a real 2.4 million-acre trackless wilderness. The landscape is truly breathtaking. The fishing is technical and difficult. One year it was below zero, the wind was blowing, it was snowing sideways, and the Sisters didn't catch anything. When the Sisters got back to their hotel (it was too cold for trailer camping), they set up a "no-campfire campfire." They sat in a circle, drinking whiskey out of the bottle for warmth and taking turns rubbing one another's frozen feet.

Around the campfire, the Sisters talk about the time that two Sisters (one at each end of a boat) caught the same fish; about the time two Sisters, again one at each end of the boat, each caught a fish at the same time and the guide didn't know which fish to net first; and about catching and eating fresh crab on the Oregon coast. ("Did that count as fishing?" the Sisters wonder.)

But the best stories are always about the amazing Mazie. When Mazie goes out fishing, someone has to be in charge of her. Why? Because she would stay out all day and never come home. One day, on the Madison River in Montana, the rain was coming down in sheets. Mazie

TOP: Who needs traditional waders? Ferne Krumm (Sister #28) is one of a dozen or more Sisters who regularly fish in a skirt.

BOTTOM: Mazie, the flies for the day's fishing securely fastened to her Sisters on the Fly cap, is ready to head out onto the river.

was soaked to the skin (why she never gets sick is anyone's guess), but she was too busy fishing to notice. Maurrie (Sister #1) waded out into the stream with a big black garbage bag to make a raincoat for her mom. "Do you want to come in out of the rain?" Maurrie asked.

Before we tell you Mazie's response, we should digress for a moment to note that Mazie acquired her taste for salty language by being married to a U.S. Marine for fifty-three years. "What the hell are you talking about? I'm putting on this raincoat and staying right here. The fishing is great," she says.

This is why the Sisters call her the amazing Mazie. The lesson learned: Go fishing. You'll live longer and your life will be more fun.

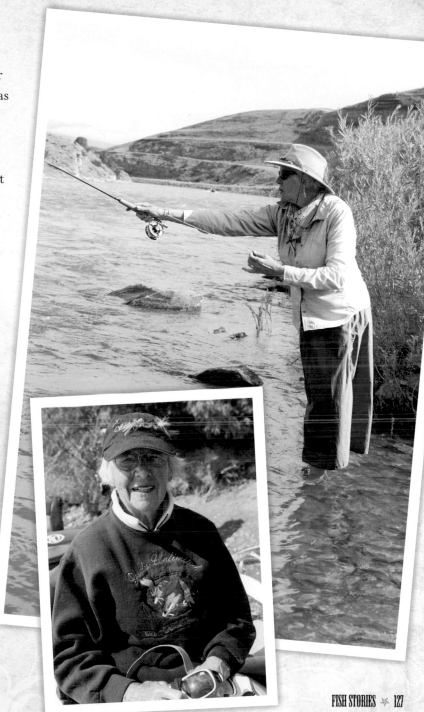

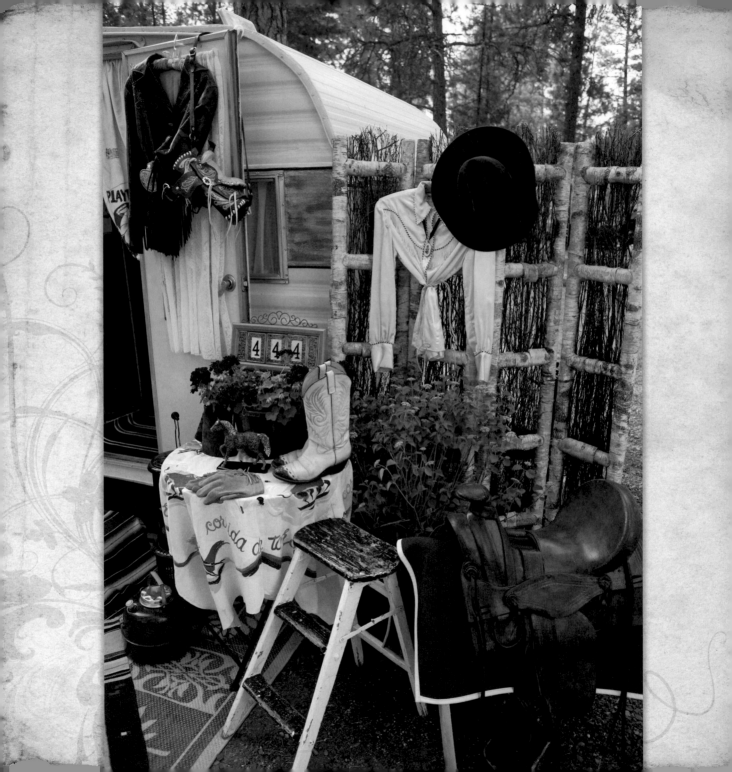

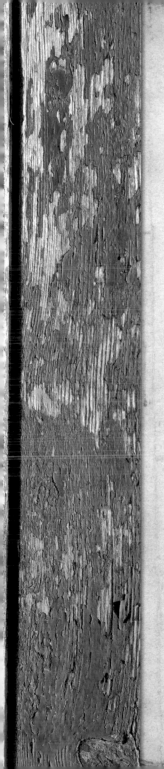

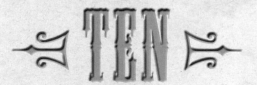 TEN

CAMPING COLLECTIBLES

Most everyone collects something—from matchbooks and bottles to vintage linens and fishing creels. The Sisters are no exception. They love to decorate and to "stage" their trailers. They buy colorful Pendleton camp blankets, vintage Tres Outlaws cowboy boots, and antique Haida fishing creels. They love to shop—singly or in a group—for the perfect flea-market finds to furnish their trailers, which, many say, are like dollhouses.

"It certainly feels like playing house," says Becky. "Now that I have three trailers, it is fun to decorate each one differently, and I can decorate trailers quicker, easier, and cheaper than I could do with a house."

Cheri Macdonald (Sister #802) agrees. Her 1966 Scotty Tonga is her plaything—a big toy house—that she's furnishing in fly-fishing and tea-drinking collectibles. "Sometimes I just go sit in my trailer," she says. "If my husband can't find me, he knows to come out into the garage and look in the trailer and there I'll be."

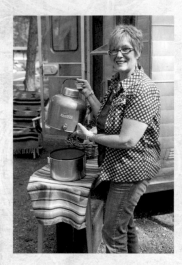

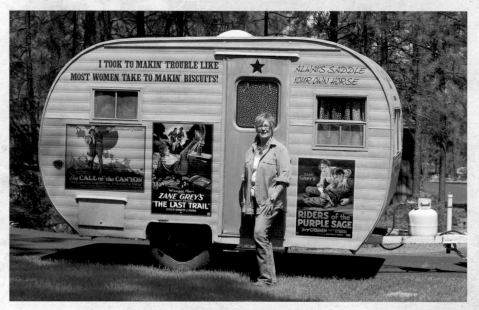

PREVIOUS: A birch and willow screen hides the "business end" of the trailer, while a collection of Western accessories tells everyone that a real cowgirl lives here.

ABOVE: Teresa Klocke (Sister #430) shows off a vintage canteen, designed to keep beverages cool on a camping trip. The bottom (on the table) opens up for ice.

TOP RIGHT: After Teresa Klocke discovered she was related to the legendary novelist Zane Grey, shopping for her trailer decor became easy. She decorates the 1960 Winnebago—inside and out—with posters from old Westerns.

BOTTOM RIGHT: An old Coca-Cola ice chest is as practical as it is adorable.

Teresa Klocke (Sister #430) decorates her trailer, a 1960 Winnebago, in a Zane Grey *Riders of the Purple Sage* motif. "I was working on my genealogy and discovered that I'm related to Zane Grey through a mutual ancestor, Colonel Ebenezer Zane," she says. As a result, she's always on the lookout for anything Zane Grey, especially books and movie posters.

Childhood fantasies often come to life in these little trailers. Glenda Stone (Sister #62), who has a 1969 Scotty, went to Cowgirl College a "shy housewife and came out a self-assured woman." She takes her 1951 Lucy doll on the Sisters trips. "The doll was bought when I was born," she says. "She has

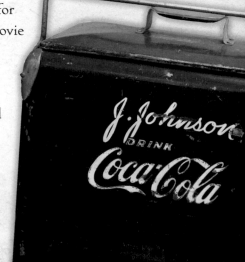

her own suitcase and loves to travel." Glenda, known to the Sisters as "G!" scouts the tag sales for clothes and accessories for her Lucy doll.

Sweet Fannie Magee, a 1963 Metzendorf (supposedly made of sheets of metal that were used to make tin cans), belongs to antiques dealer Sharon Lambert (Sister #508). Because Sweet Fannie is a "Southern lady trailer," she requires more refined furnishings, such as a crystal chandelier above the dinette table. Sharon has a network of dealer friends who are always on the lookout for charming antiques with a Southern lineage that are small enough to suit Sweet Fannie.

Tani Gibson (Sister #120) decorates very simply: She hangs up her boots, chaps, and spurs. Sue Wenner (Sister #556), who plays a hundred-year-old fiddle, has a dual theme—cowgirls and music. In her trailer, she carries an antique banjo and other vintage musical instruments, plus a guitar made out of a bedpan and barbed wire ("It's folk art!").

Paulette Roth (Sister #249) uses color copies of old fishing postcards from the 1940s, vintage cowgirl posters, and old luggage labels to decorate her trailer. Pam Heron, aka the Queen of Pamalot (Sister #79) decorates her trailer in vintage glitter and Hollywood glitz—all found at antiques shows and garage sales.

BELOW LEFT: The boots are for riding; the vintage coal hod is used for storing ice.

BELOW: Some campgrounds don't have hookups, so vintage washbasins and chamber pots come in handy. This Sister keeps her "washing up station" just outside the door of her trailer.

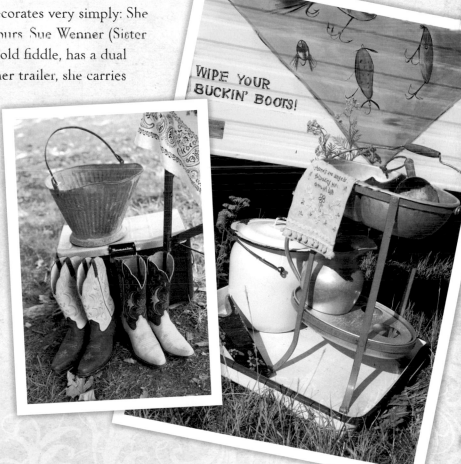

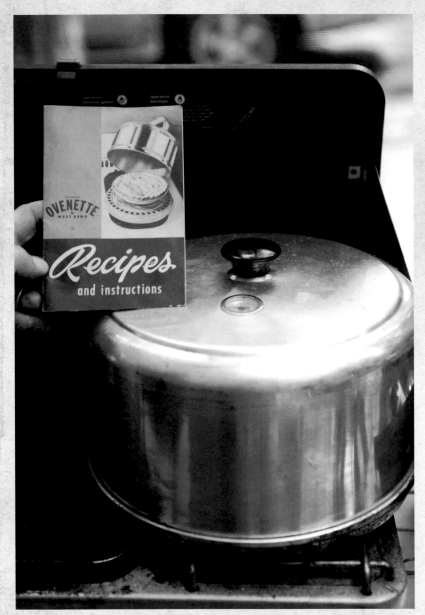

Cathy Preston (Sister #510) says of her friend Erin Healey (Sister #88), "I've never seen so much stuff glued and screwed to the walls." Erin defends her decor by saying that B. B. King played at her prom and, therefore, she's always had a fondness for blues memorabilia.

Tammy Hise (Sister #683) collects fabric and contact paper from the 1960s to use in her 1968 Fireball. Kaarin Simpson (Sister #441) hunts for 1940s Mexican collectibles for her 1965 Shasta, Cowgirl Cantina. Antique camping kitchenware, especially anything in workable condition that comes with its original instruction book, is a must-buy for Beverly Brand (Sister #615), who uses her finds to cook dinner on the road, much to the delight of her other Sisters.

And the most wonderful thing about personal collections: There are more than 1,300 Sisters and every single trailer is different.

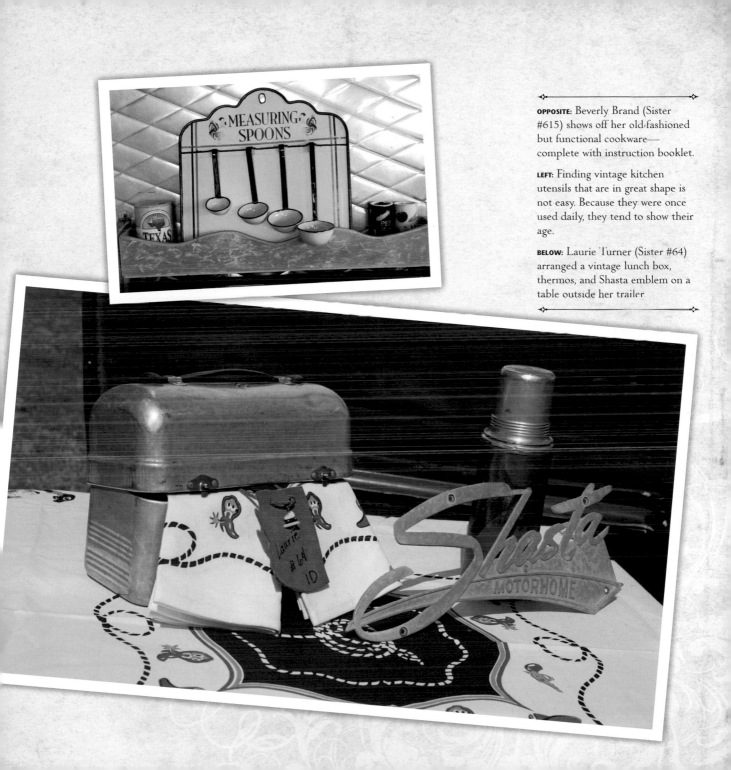

OPPOSITE: Beverly Brand (Sister #615) shows off her old-fashioned but functional cookware—complete with instruction booklet.

LEFT: Finding vintage kitchen utensils that are in great shape is not easy. Because they were once used daily, they tend to show their age.

BELOW: Laurie Turner (Sister #64) arranged a vintage lunch box, thermos, and Shasta emblem on a table outside her trailer.

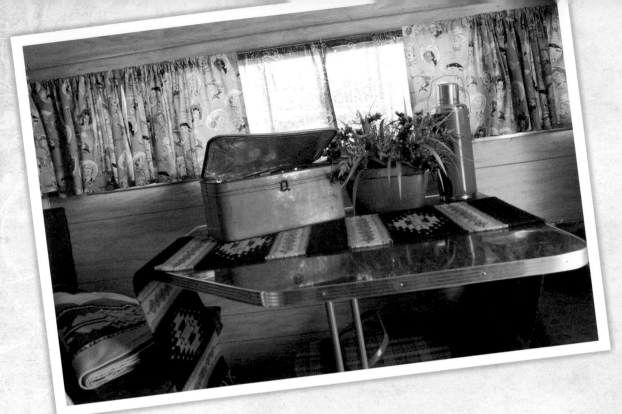

HOW TO STAGE YOUR TRAILER

ABOVE: A tin bread box (showing some wear), a peach-colored thermos, a plaid picnic basket, and some vintage blankets decorate the dinette of this Sister's trailer.

OPPOSITE TOP: "Staging" your trailer with vintage items is a way to welcome visitors and create a true home away from home. Julie Thorson (Sister #444), the editor of *Horse & Rider* magazine, knows how to stage a trailer.

OPPOSITE BOTTOM: Julie always has her collection of vintage Western romance novels on display and is happy to lend them out.

If you are a true collector, you never stop collecting. So what do you do when you run out of room? If you're a Sister, you use the outdoors as an extension of your trailer's inside living space. In other words, you "stage" your trailer.

Here's how: Sisters know that everyday objects come to life when placed in a stage-type setting. A wooden ironing board becomes a vintage tablecloth-draped bar. A school chalkboard on a metal stand becomes a table that doubles as a message board: "Gone to town. Back soon." A rusted porch chair gets a new coat of paint and "Sisters on the Fly" stenciled on the back of it. An abandoned garden gate becomes a backdrop for pots of fresh flowers. Martini bars—the kind that come with chrome shakers and their own little traveling cases—are much in demand. Camping gear, useful or merely decorative, is a must both inside and outside every Sister's trailer.

Julie Thorson (Sister #444), the editor of *Horse & Rider*, is an accomplished trailer stager. "The moment I arrive at a camping spot, I start setting up," she says.

First, she sets up an aspen-and-twig screen to hide "the business end" of the trailer—the hitch and the propane tank. Then she sets up her ironing-board bar "in case the sun is

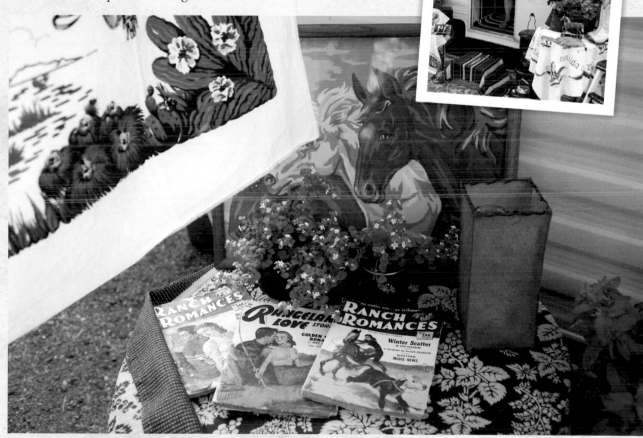

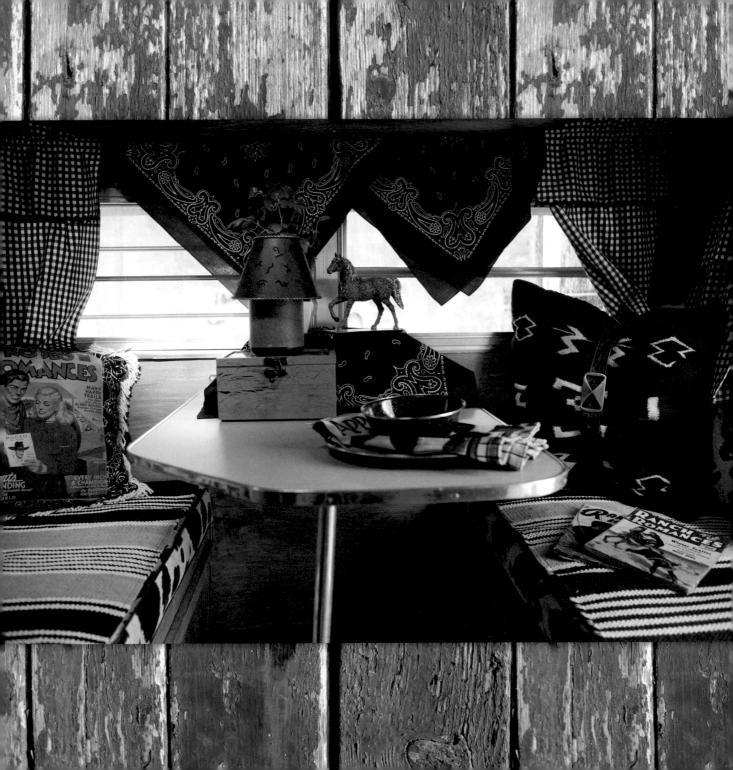

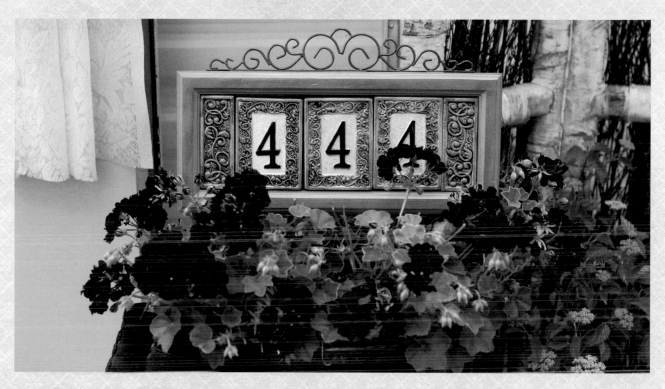

high in the sky and one—or more—of the Sisters wants to come over for a drink." Her collection of Western-themed romances is displayed prominently on a little table just outside her trailer's door. "They are collectibles, sure, but if a Sister wants to take one to read . . . that's just fine," she says.

On the way to the camping spot, she will have stopped at a grocery store or garden center for fresh plants—geraniums and herbs are her favorites. "One's beautiful, the other's useful," she says. Staging complete, she walks around the campsite to lend a hand and to see what the other Sisters have collected since their last rendezvous. "It is really a time to show off a little . . . to shine," she says.

OPPOSITE: Inside Julie's trailer (a 1972 Scotty that she found on eBay), the Western theme continues with tin dishware and old-fashioned kerchiefs as simple window coverings.

ABOVE: A charming house-number plaque proudly announces Julie's Sister number, while fresh geraniums add color and beauty.

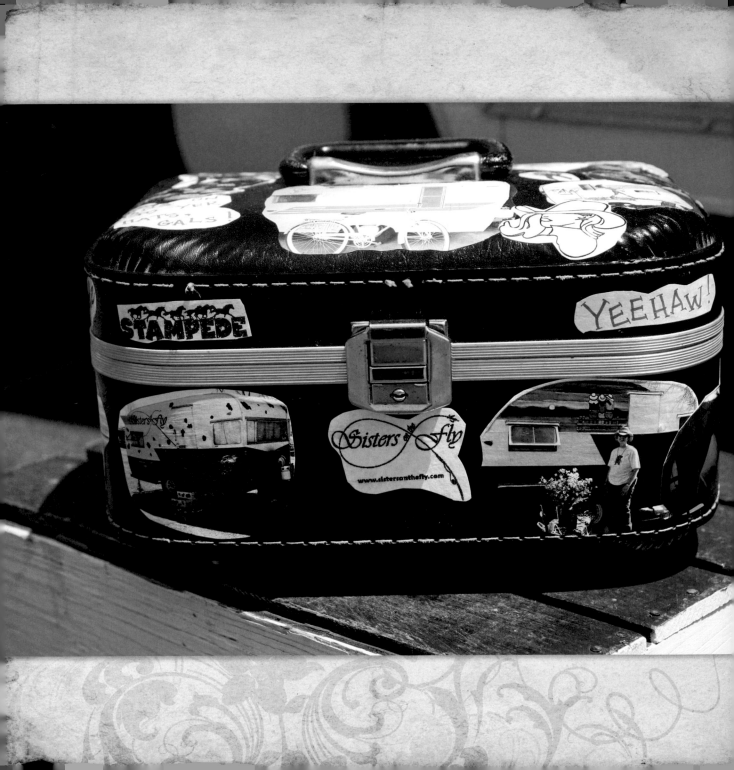

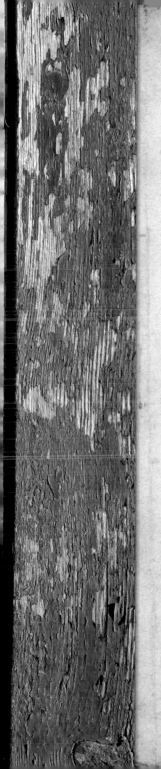

≈ ELEVEN ≈

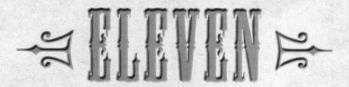

COWGIRL CRAFTS

From slipcovers and curtains to quilting and calligraphy, the Sisters are a handy bunch, and it shows—in their homes, their trailers, and the gifts they make for one another.

FOR THE KITCHEN

Because potluck suppers are such a big part of Sisters events, Anita Wallace (Sister #440) has designed and decorated a double-handled casserole carrier with a cowgirl/trailer motif. She sells these at Sisters events, with the proceeds going to charity. Her trailer-themed dish towels and cowgirl scarves are also a big hit. "I always have a project going," she says with a laugh. "Well . . . more than one project. One for home and one I can work on while I'm the road—not while I'm driving, of course."

Anita's dish towels are easy to make. Take a piece of absorbent fabric—cotton, linen, or terry cloth are best—and cut it to measure about 17 x 28 inches. Don't fuss about getting the size exact. Hem the edges. Cut a little roundish trailer-shaped piece from a contrasting fabric. Machine appliqué it to the towel. Make a little door out of another cute fabric. Appliqué it to the little trailer. Use a vintage button for the wheel and a small pearl button or bead for the doorknob on the little trailer's door. They end up almost too cute to use, but Anita says they're washable, so go ahead.

Many Sisters collect aprons, make aprons, and belong to apron exchanges. Grace Brown (Sister #473) is an exceptional needlewoman and makes aprons for all the Sisters. She says it is easy—and she's right.

Take one yard of 45-inch washable fabric. Vintage fabrics such as bark cloth are perfect. From one end, cut two 9 x 37-inch pieces for the tie belt and one 9 x 24-inch piece for the waistband (which will measure 4 1/2 inches when folded over). The rest of the fabric is the body of the apron.

Fold ties with the right sides together, stitch, turn, and press. Make a hem on the bottom of the apron (the other two sides will be the selvage edges). Gather the apron. Sew the waistband onto the right side of the apron (right side of apron to right side of waistband). Tuck the ties into each end of the waistband and sew. Straight lines. Straight cuts. Easy sewing.

SISTERS QUILTS

Quilts are made quickly and easily—with all the Sisters on the trip participating to the extent of their abilities. At the California Dreamin' event, word filters through from one Sister to the next that a Sister is ill or another Sister has lost her husband. Squares of muslin come out, along with permanent markers in rainbow colors. Pretty soon, the Sisters are sitting at picnic tables drawing pictures—some as simple as a big grinning sun with rays reaching down to the earth, others complicated renditions of trailers in the woods with a trout stream winking and twinkling in the near distance.

When each Sister has drawn a picture or written an inspirational message, one of the Sisters takes the quilt pieces home to sew them together, add batting and a back, and do the quilting—by hand or machine, depending on her skills. The finished quilts are a joy to behold. Each one is different, and each one is welcomed by the recipient as a sign of hope and token of love.

TRAVELING LOVE QUILTS

Because the quilts are so appreciated, Maurrie started a project called the Traveling Love Quilt. One of her favorite pastimes is to look in antiques stores for old quilt tops and quilt pieces that "have been hanging around for a few years with no one wanting them." She gathers them up (some are lovely, some are ugly), repairs them, and brings them back to life because, in each piece, she sees the love put into them by someone sitting in front of an old sewing machine or stitching them by hand.

One of the Sisters who got a Love Quilt had breast cancer, and she

One of the Sisters always carries squares of muslin and a box full of embroidery thread and permanent markers so the Sisters can, at a moment's notice, create a friendship pillow or the squares for a quilt.

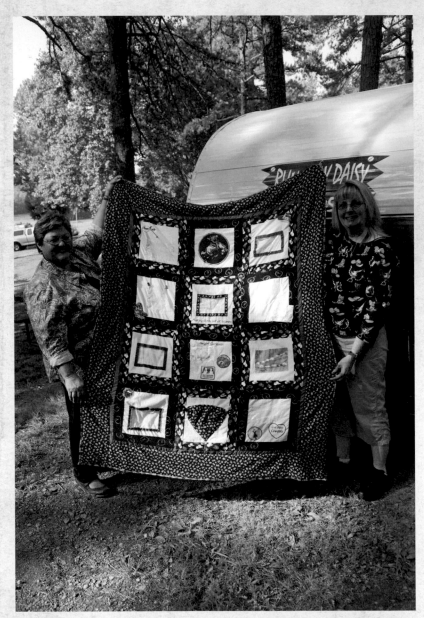

took the quilt to chemo with her. When she went into remission and no longer needed the quilt to keep her warm, she came up with an idea. Why not pass the quilt along to someone else who needs it? So, when the quilts are no longer needed, they come back to Maurrie, who cleans and repairs them. They are then passed on from Sister to Sister—on and on—to provide "tons of love to wrap around you so you know that, even though we are not physically with you, we are emotionally there with our arms wrapped around you."

FOR YOUR TRAILER

For all her work with quilts, Maurrie is handier with a fly rod than a needle, but she makes the curtains in all her trailers, and she makes sure they are lined so "they look as pretty from the outside as they do from the inside." That's a good tip for any home.

Friendship pillows—shaped like hearts, cowgirl boots, chaps,

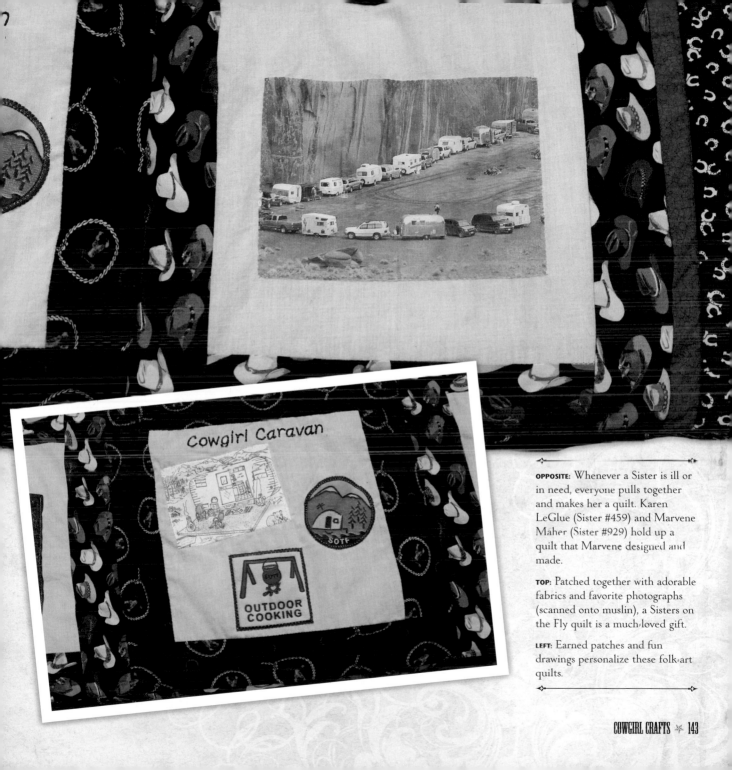

OPPOSITE: Whenever a Sister is ill or in need, everyone pulls together and makes her a quilt. Karen LeGlue (Sister #459) and Marvene Maher (Sister #929) hold up a quilt that Marvene designed and made.

TOP: Patched together with adorable fabrics and favorite photographs (scanned onto muslin), a Sisters on the Fly quilt is a much-loved gift.

LEFT: Earned patches and fun drawings personalize these folk-art quilts.

or just plain squares—are easy to make and perfect when there's no time to make a quilt. Use a large muslin square for the front, decorate it with permanent marker, and appliqué it to the pillow. Stuff the pillow. Sew up the opening and you're done. Some of the Sisters will put a little sachet of lavender or lemon verbena inside the pillow to make it smell good. LaVerne Parnell (Sister #497) makes her pillows with transfers of old-time photographs and doesn't skimp on the lace and fringe.

Every trailer needs a stick horse. These easy-to-make toy horses hark back to the days long before any of the Sisters were born when wagons and trailers were pulled by real horses. These days, the Sisters simply display their stick horses in front of their trailers. Some Sisters decorate the horses with satin and lace and Mardi Gras beads, then ride them around the campfire while telling tales of the Wild West.

To make your own, you'll need a dowel about 2 inches in diameter and 36 inches long (painted to match the fabric), fabric for the head, and yarn for the mane. Trace the shape of a horse's head on a piece of paper to use as a pattern. Don't worry: Most of the horses' heads are shaped pretty much like a man's sock. Cut the horse's head out of fabric. Cut little pointy horsey ears out of the same fabric. Make eyes out of felt, and appliqué or glue them onto each side of the head. You can also use googly eyes.

Sew the two pieces of fabric together to make the horse's head, and stuff it. Stick the dowel into the horse's head and glue

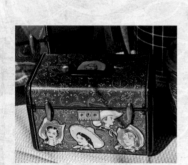

ABOVE: Since everyone needs a travel case, why not have some fun with it? Sisters find old suitcases and train cases at thrift shops and then decorate them with paper and stickers.

RIGHT: Nearly every Sister has one of these easy-to-make stick horses. Some are basic (like this one); others are decorated with rhinestone beads, feathers, and lace.

the bottom of it. Glue ears to the top of the horse's head, and glue a nice, full yarn mane between the ears and down the horse's neck. Some Sisters add cute little wheels to the bottom of the dowel.

GIFTS TO GIVE OR TO KEEP FOR YOURSELF

Most Sisters have suitcases or train cases—decoupaged with pictures and aphorisms—that they really use for travel or to schlep makeup, shampoo, and hairdryers to and from campground showers. It's easy to find old hard-sided suitcases at thrift stores or garage sales, and it's fun to customize them.

Assemble your pictures and decals, and don't forget little gold or silver letters to personalize your suitcase or train case. Play with the layout on your suitcase until it looks the way you want it to. Then, following the instructions on a bottle of decoupage glue, just glue your decorations down and seal them.

If you're doing a large project, you can save money by making your own glue. Mix white wood glue from your local hardware store (it comes in a big bucket and is used by carpenters) with water in a 1:1 ratio for gluing and 3:1 (glue:water) ratio for sealing.

Anita Wallace (Sister #440) makes fleece scarves for the Sisters and promises they are very simple to make. Choose a fleece that you like (she uses fabric with a horse or cowgirl pattern). Use sharp scissors to cut an 8-inch-wide piece (from selvage edge to selvage edge). Then cut fringe into each of the edges. If your sewing machine has an embroidery function, you can write something like "God Bless Cowgirls" or "Sisters Are

BELOW TOP: Every Sister brings her scrapbook to work on and share. Filled with photographs, drawings, quotes, and notes from other Sisters, these books are cherished keepsakes.

BELOW: Patterned paper, stickers, and markers turn any notebook into an inspired scrapbook with tons of cowgirl personality.

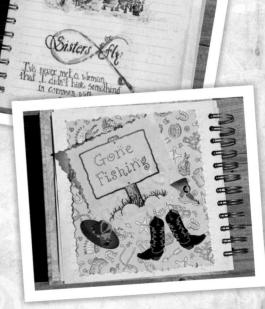

Forever" on the scarf. Bind off the raw edges with a zigzag stitch or, if you have the time, by hand with a traditional blanket stitch.

Knitted fingerless gloves are both beautiful and useful for fishing in cold weather. Joyce LeDuke (Sister #425) makes them, offers them for sale, and shares her pattern.

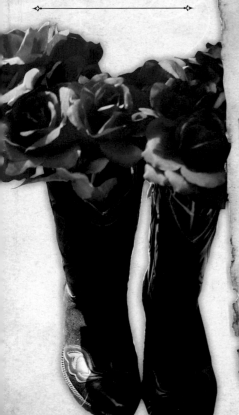

Ladies Medium Size Gloves

Materials

Less than 1 skein yarn (a great use for those bits of leftover yarn)
Size 8 and size 6 straight needles

Using size 6 needles, cast on 32 sts and 2 x 2 ribbing for 14 rows. (Note: 2 x 2 ribbing is knit 2, purl 2 every row.)

Change to size 8 needles and st st for 12 rows. (Note: st st [stockinette stitch] is knit right side row, purl wrong side row.)

Change to size 6 needles and 2 x 2 rib for 14 rows.

Cast off next row in ribbing, leaving a long tail to sew seam.

Fold edges together (with ribbing at top and bottom) and sew ribbed section together plus 4 stitches into stockinette st area.

Fasten off.

Thumb hole: Attach yarn approximately 6 sts from end of seam on right side of work. Pick up 6 sts on one side of seam and 6 sts on other side of seam. Then 2 x 2 rib on these 12 sts for one row, then bind off in rib, leaving long tail to finish seam.

Sew thumb hole and rest of side seam. And you're done.

SISTERHOOD SCRAPBOOKS

Sisterhood scrapbooks are a given. Every Sister has one and brings it to Cowgirl Caravan events—to work on in the evenings and to share her photographs, stickers, artwork, recipes, remedies, or little snippets of poetry or advice. Sisters ask Sisters to do a little drawing, write a little something, or share a recipe as they sit around the campfire at day's end. Some scrapbooks get a little singed or—oh darn!—get a little wine or coffee spilled on them, but that only adds to their already considerable charm.

Give Katie Quinn (Sister #1033) a moment and she'll pen some poetry on your page. She often says, "Laughter from the heart is good for the soul."

a fly drops gently
on the river's clear waters
fish strikes hook is set

Ferne Krumm (Sister #28) will almost certainly also write something poetic—something about "the river . . . a ribbon winding . . . always changing . . . full of fish . . . sunlight sparkling on the water."

It is what every Sister dreams of when she's dropping off to sleep miles away from her other Sisters—or close by, each in her cozy trailer.

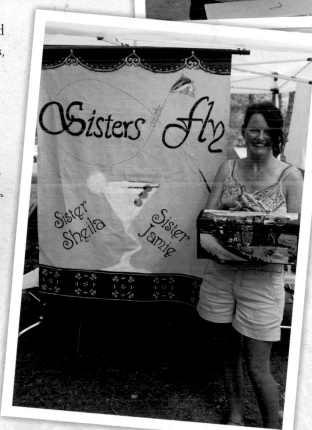

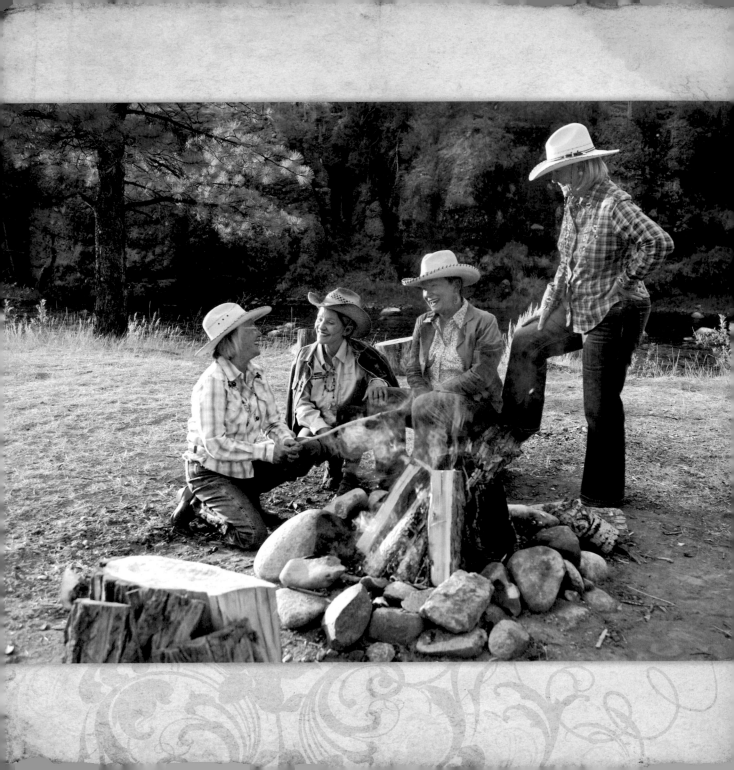

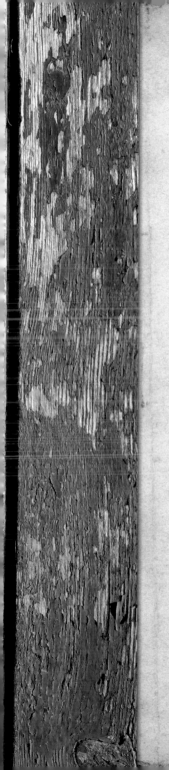

TWELVE

STORIES AND SONGS

On a clear night under a blanket of stars, the dark sky opens up its treasure chest and invites you to take a look. Lying, perhaps for the first time since childhood, in a cool alfalfa-scented field with your Sisters, you gaze into the night sky, and it seems that the stars are a brilliant mass of crushed diamonds sprinkled across a velvet backdrop.

One is pulled out of place by a mysterious force that causes it to go streaking from its home. Shooting star! Silence follows as everyone remembers they are supposed to make a wish on that shooting star and hopes it is not too late. Constellations, brilliant and intriguing, are traced with fingertips, and the darkness of the vast night sky makes them seem like faraway ancient petroglyphs.

Whether lying out in a cool alfalfa field or sitting around a blazing campfire, Sisters on the Fly always have stories to tell. Sometimes they are heroic tales about landing a big brown trout;

sometimes they are ghost stories. Other times they are simple stories about life, love, children, and grandchildren.

Here's a favorite story told in hushed tones around the campfire: Maurrie was fishing on the Gallatin River; she missed her footing and started sinking in quicksand. Another Sister rushed in to save her but also started sinking. Although everyone remembers that Maurrie was laughing, both Sisters were truly sinking into the quicksand. Finally, someone rushed to the back of one of the pickups, pulled out some long boards, and slid them toward the sinking Sisters, who were then able to sit on the boards and very slowly pull themselves out. According to Maurrie, the moral of the story is this: When a Sister is in trouble, don't jump in feet first. Use your head to figure out what's best.

Another Sister leans forward, puts her elbows on her knees, and starts talking. She tells of an older brother who picked on her relentlessly. He was notorious for tormenting his little sister. But since he was much older, it didn't take long before she was, basically, an only child. She talks about longing for a sister her entire life and the joy of finding such a wonderful group of women. No matter how many miles are between them or how many days have passed since the Sisters last met, their conversations pick up just where they had left off, she remarks. Much happy laughter follows this story.

A Sister who has been having some serious health problems starts talking. The laughter stops; everyone listens intently. She says that when the sheer weight of the world is heavy on your mind and you don't want to cry in front of your husband, your horse is waiting to be hugged. He doesn't mind if you cling to his neck and sob into his mane. He doesn't get panicky because you are bawling; he just stands patiently, wondering why you are making all those funny noises. It is truly the best therapy a girl can have, besides confiding in a Sister or a dear friend. The simple act of being with a horse calms the mind. When you climb on a horse and the wind is blowing through your hair, you can forget your worries and just enjoy being alive. Silently, the Sisters nod and hug one another close.

Someone tells the story about Mazie and the big blond grizzly bear that was so close she could see the color of his eyes (which were, by the way, a nice golden brown). There are tales about the naked river guide (don't ask); the night a herd of elk bedded down right next to the Sisters' encampment; and a local fisherman up at the Henry's Fork River in Idaho who overstayed his welcome and got a little too friendly for comfort. He was told in no uncertain terms that the Sisters were "packin'" and if he tried to set one foot inside any one of the trailers, he would be shot. He left in a hurry, never to return.

The Southern Sisters are especially adept at telling stories because they understand that it's the kiss of death to start a story at the beginning. They know how to start in the middle and add layer after layer, always with some new little addition. "It comes from those long summer evenings before air-conditioning when it was too hot to sit inside and everyone sat out on the porch listening to the best storytellers in the county," says Anita Wallace (Sister #440).

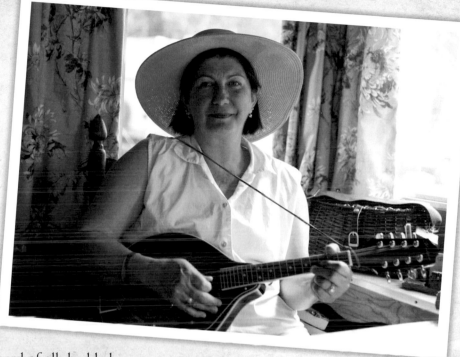

PREVIOUS: A well-built campfire along the river's edge always encourages good storytelling and lots of fish tales. Maurrie Sussman (Sister #1), who learned the art of telling a good fish story from her mother, Mazie (Sister #4), holds everyone's attention.

ABOVE: Rhonda Gamble (Sister #1063) sits in her 1958 Kenskill trailer, tuning up for the evening's songfest.

Southern Sisters are also famous for their old wives' remedies—for everything from making your cat hypoallergenic (rub it down with Listerine) to rinsing your pillowcases with lavender water to promote sleep and sweet dreams. They also enjoy rip-snorting ghost stories.

One Sister swears she has an antebellum ghost, a lady in a long green dress, who floats into the dining room at night and drinks all the sherry in the decanter on the sideboard. The Sisters laugh and playfully accuse the storyteller of sleepwalking. Another is sure she nearly hit a Confederate soldier ghost with her car on a lonely stretch of country road between Beaufort and Lands End, South Carolina. Still another talks about a recent sighting of Gray Man, who, so they say, has appeared on the beach at Pawleys Island for more than a hundred years. The Sisters nod in remembrance. This is an oft-told story.

One of the musical Sisters elicits gasps when she tells about taking her guitar to the junction of U.S. 61 and U.S. 49 in the Mississippi Delta, the very same crossroads where, legend has it, blues guitarist Robert Johnson sold his soul to the devil. So what happened? Evidently, there were already nearly a dozen other musicians sitting there with their guitars "waiting to see what would happen," and finally they just started to play—right out there in the pitch-black rural Mississippi night. No devil. Just a good jam session.

COWGIRL POETS

With so many Sisters experiencing once-in-a-lifetime adventures (not to mention the many who keep journals) it's no wonder that several are moved to write poetry.

Cowgirl Sisters

The truck bumps and lurches as it shimmies along the hardpan road. Ruts wind thru tufts of laymans lovegrass. Mesquite trees dot pastures, sharing space with a herd of Angus. Dirt devils dance between the steer's legs.

Memories swirl.

Every trailer circled in the camp exposes the soul of the sister nestled within. Each is finished with abandon and love. A gnarled, bent Mexican oak tree is festooned in garlands of twinkle lights. It mimics the stars glowing above the high desert sky.

Memories swirl.

The old chuckwagon groans under its heavy load of food. Sisters all gather round the campfire. Their laughter echoes through the cold night air, only rivaled by the coyotes howling at the moon.

Memories swirl.

Snug inside our vintage traveling homes, buried under layers of quilts, I smile. I'm thinking about the sisters, all so amazing, so genuine and, shhhhh! so moxy (not to mention they're also foxy). Each sister evolves, anchored to the earth while reaching for the sky.

Memories fly.

❖ *Betsy Snyder (Sister #1001)*

And Why Not?

I try to convey to my friends who will say, "Why do you go off on those trips? You sleep in the wild with no plumbing or water. You either freeze or your skin's never hotter. What makes roughing it so appealing?"

Don't they know, can't they see? It's the only time I get to be me! All decorum is gone in the wink of an eye. I'm riding a horse and I'm ready to fly! Or I might wade with a trout on my line in a cold mountain stream—so cold I could scream.

Just gathered round the campfire, the soles of my boots searing, a sister tells an anecdote and we're suddenly all cheering. Surrounded by Sisters, I feel myself growing, enlivened, challenged. I go home glowing.

Each time I swing up into my own vintage trailer, it's a coming home moment. My DNA's all over the space from curtains I made, to the floor that I laid. From my flea market finds, to the quilt I designed.

There's no "if ands or buts," the good is all there! Now would you mind, just this once, pull me up outta this chair? (I'm not as young as I used to be!)

❧ Betsy Snyder (Sister #1001)

Sisters on the Fly

Vintage trailer decorating
Camping in the wood together
Cowgirls riding horses, ye'haw!

Fly-fishing dreams float down the streams,
Kayaks bob around the bend
Zip-line screams above the trees.

Sisters do it all.
Helping women to be girls again.

Using up the day,
They laugh around the fires,
Toasting until all are tired.

Giving to those in need,
Sharing hearts plant a seed.

They are Sisters on the Fly
Of which one is I!!

✦ *Sally Y. Weber (Sister #951)*

SINGING SISTERS

Many of the Sisters bring their guitars, banjos, and mandolins to the gatherings and play traditional camp songs that speak of love, loss, and lament. Sometimes they play popular country songs, the ones that extol the virtues of a simple life. A perennial favorite is Rosemary and Betty Clooney's 1950s hit "Sisters"—especially the part about caring and sharing.

As the campfire burns itself to embers, someone breaks into song—maybe a familiar but barely remembered song learned at camp years

Sue Wenner (Sister #556) stands in front of Pickin' Palace, a trailer she shares with her daughters Andi Wenner (Sister #572) and Melinda Wenner (Sister #573). She recently retired as a teacher of English as a second language to concentrate on perfecting her fiddling talents.

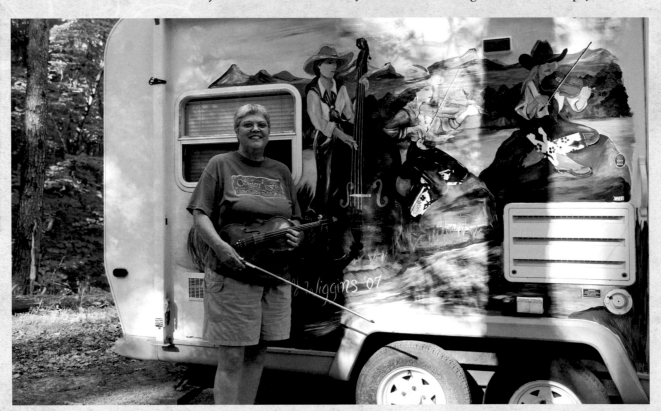

before. Other Sisters join in. Only a few are in tune, but no one seems to mind, and, oddly enough, it sounds pretty darn good. Then one of the Sisters picks up a guitar and another one a mandolin and soon there are more toasts and singing around the campfire.

But the Sisters have also had songs written about them. Bob Haworth, who toured for nearly four decades as a key member of the Brothers Four and the Kingston Trio, has written a song about Sisters on the Fly. Here's an excerpt. You can hear more at http://www.bobhaworth.com/rvsongs.html and download it to your iPod. Proceeds benefit ALS, Parkinson's, and Alzheimer's research.

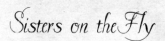

Sisters on the Fly

They're modern-day cowgirls out on the open road,
Vintage trailer caravans and hearts as pure as gold.
Looking for adventure and a rainbow trout to fry.
They're modern-day cowgirls . . . they're Sisters on the Fly.
Sisters on the Fly . . . riding wild and riding high.
They have more fun than anyone . . . they're Sisters on the Fly.

ABOVE: Rhonda Gamble (Sister #1063) and Sue Wenner (Sister #556) sit down and play old favorites—songs from the trail, sweet songs of love, and fondly remembered folk tunes. Pretty soon, the Sisters have gathered around, joining in and making requests.

NEXT: Evening campfires are always a must, as are sweet and gooey roasted marshmallows and lots of stories and songs.

AND TO ALL A GOOD NIGHT

Darkness falls. The stars are too numerous to count but seem close enough to touch. A log crackles and flares up, momentarily casting light

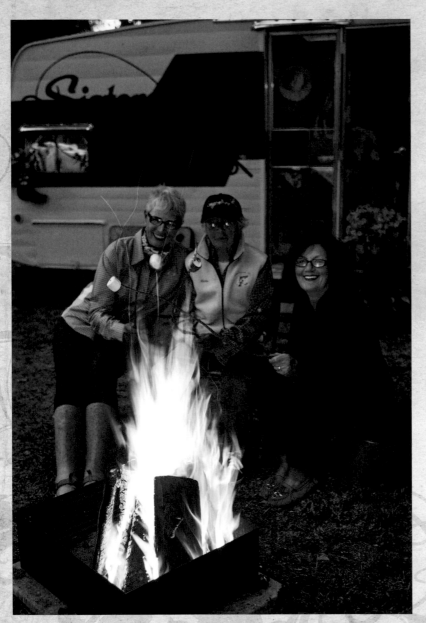

on the faces of the Sisters closest to the fire. An owl hoots in the tree nearby. A coyote barks in the distance. One more song and one more story.

"Tell the one about the prospector led to safety by a beautiful ghost," asks one Sister.

"No, the one about the couple parked in Lover's Lane and the escaped convict with a hook for an arm," asks another.

"I heard he had the hook on his foot," says another, and everyone laughs.

Finally, the Sisters say their goodnights and head off to bed, each sinking into the soft featherbed inside her cozy cowgirl trailer. Maybe she'll dream about fishing, sisterhood, or the open road. But chances are she'll be asleep before her head even hits the pillow. Fresh air does that.

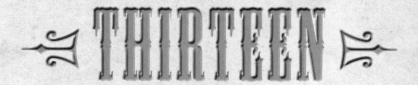

THIRTEEN

RESOURCES

Web sites to see, books to read, and other good stuff . . . plus places to get tools for the trip.

VINTAGE TRAILERS

http://www.airstreamtrailers.com
http://www.americanvintagerv.com
http://www.montanacampsandcabins.com
http://www.sistersonthefly.com
http://www.tincantourists.com//classified
http://www.vintagecampers.com
http://www.vintagetrailercrazy.com
http://www.vintage-vacations.com

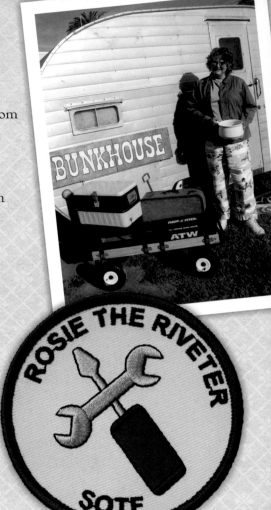

Fixin' It Up

http://www.montanacampsandcabins.com
http://www.retrorestoration.com
http://www.timelesstraveltrailers.com
http://www.vintagetrailersupply.com
http://www.ynotcamperrestoration.com

Decoratin' It

http://www.amberjean.com
http://www.chapmandesigninc.com
http://www.colleendrury.com
http://www.dancinglightlamps.com
http://www.ddranchwear.com
http://www.fallriverrustics.com
http://www.glasshorsestudio.com
http://www.indiancreekleather.com
http://www.jfhudson.com
http://www.jillhartleystudio.com
http://www.jkbrand.com
http://www.luckystargallery.com
http://www.melindalutke.com
http://www.reflectionsofjoi.com
http://www.rosemariegallery.com
http://www.roundtoptexasantiques.com/shows.html
http://www.rusticfurniture.net
http://www.supayagraywolfe.com
http://www.thalglass.com
http://www.thefarmchicks.com/show.html

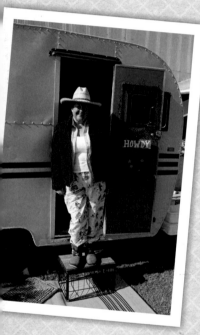

http://www.thesalvagestudio.com
http://www.westernfurnishings.com
http://www.westernware.net

TRAVEL TOOLS

Practical
http://coleman.com
http://solardirect.com (solar shower)
http://www.campingworld.com
http://www.rei.com

Vintage/Fun
http://www.bestinhome.com
http://www.nostalgiafactoryoutlet.com

ALL ABOUT FISHING

http://www.catchmagazine.net
http://www.deepcreekflyfishers.org
http://www.flymaxfilms.com
http://www.garybulla.com
http://www.seaandstreamflyfishing.com
http://www.montanaflyfishingoutfitter.com

Women Fly Fishers
http://reel-women.com
http://www.intlwomenflyfishers.org

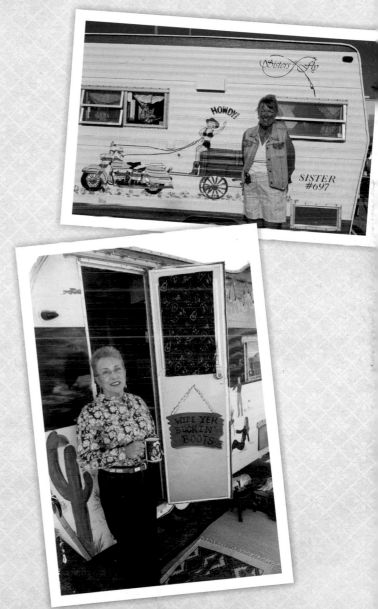

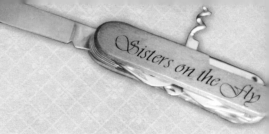

Sisters on the Fly

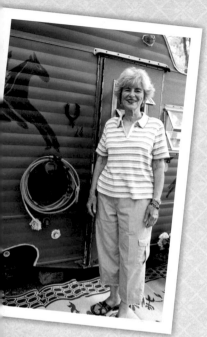

http://www.womeninthestream.com
http://www.womensflyfishing.net

Fly-fishing Gear for Girls
http://www.charbloom.com
http://www.dan-bailey.com
http://www.flyfishusa.com/women/women.htm
http://www.macabiskirt.com
http://www.roundrocks.com
http://www.superflyfishing.com/womenflyfishing.html

COWGIRL CHIC

http://www.ahootenanny.com
http://www.clairsaddleshop.com
http://www.cowgirlbootmaker.com
http://www.ddranchwear.com
http://www.denicelangley.com
http://www.luckystargallery.com
http://www.nativevogue.com
http://www.rodeocosmetics.com
http://www.sorrellcustomboots.com
http://www.thistleswest.com

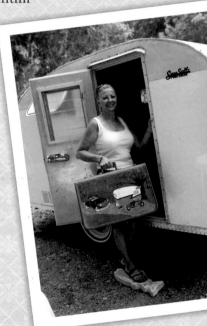

JUST FOR FUN

http://vintagetraveltrailerart.com (paintings of vintage trailers)
http://www.vroomersonline.com (slippers shaped like vintage trailers)

BLOGS

http://1947SilverLark.blogspot.com
http://graciesvictorianrose.blogspot.com
http://projectsforyournest.blogspot.com
http://thebeehivecottage.blogspot.com
http://thetincancottage.blogspot.com
http://thevintagehousewife.blogspot.com
http://vintagetraveltrailersforsale.net
http://www.apronmemories.com
http://www.maryjanesfarm.org
http://www.thefarmchicks.com
http://www.thepioneerwoman.com
http://www.TreadLightly.Org

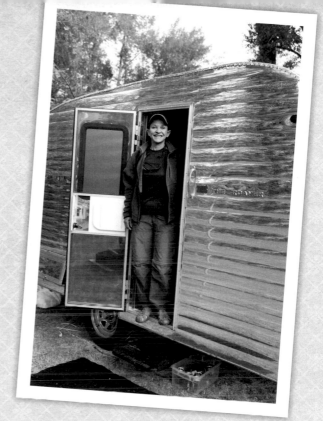

BOOKS

Abel, Mary, and Irene Rawlings. *Portable Houses.* Salt Lake City, Utah: Gibbs Smith, 2004

Bennett, Virginia, ed. *Cowgirl Poetry: One Hundred Years of Ridin' and Rhymin'.* Salt Lake City, Utah: Gibbs Smith, 2001.

Burkhart, Bryan, Phil Noyes, and Allison Arieff. *Trailer Travel: A Visual History of Mobile America.* Salt Lake City, Utah: Gibbs Smith, 2002.

Fielder, John. *Ranches of Colorado.* Boulder, Colo.: Westcliffe Publishers, 2009.

Flood, Elizabeth. *Cowgirls: Women of the Wild West.* Santa Fe, N.M.: Zon International Publishing, 1999.

Gellner, Arrol, and Douglas Keister. *Ready to Roll: A Celebration of the Classic American Travel Trailer.* New York: Viking, 2003.

Hasselstrom, Linda. *Feels Like Far: A Rancher's Life on the Great Plains.* New York: Lyons Press, 1999.

Keen, Jim, and Ami Elizabeth Reeves. *Great Ranches of the West.* Colorado Springs, Colo.: Keen Media, 2007.

Keister, Douglas. *Silver Palaces.* Salt Lake City, Utah: Gibbs Smith, 2004.

Savage, Candace Sherk. *Born to be a Cowgirl: A Spirited Ride Through the Old West.* Berkeley: Tricycle Press, 2001.

Smith, Ellen Reid. *Cowgirl Smarts: How to Rope a Kick-Ass Life.* Austin, Texas: Cowgirl Smarts Books, 2004.

Wood, Donald, *RVs & Campers: 1900 Through 2000, an Illustrated History.* Hudson, Wis.: Iconografix, 2002.

MAGAZINES

American Cowboy http://www.americancowboy.com

Cowboys & Indians http://www.cowboysindians.com

Horse & Rider http://www.equisearch.com/horseandrider

I.M. Cowgirl Magazine http://www.imcowgirl.com

MaryJanesFarm http://www.maryjanesfarm.org/magazine.html

Western Horseman http://www.westernhorseman.com

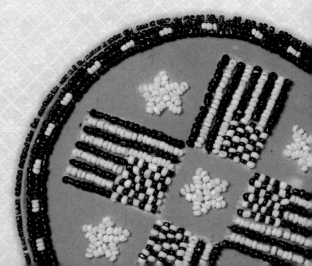

ACKNOWLEDGMENTS

Many, many thanks to Maurrie, Becky, the amazing Mazie, and all of the fabulous, independent, creative, and feisty women who make up this extraordinary group called Sisters on the Fly. You have welcomed me into your midst and have become dear friends—true sisters of my heart.

A big thanks to photographer David "Mister Sister" Foxhoven and to that intrepid cowgirl photographer Audrey Hall. She made Maurrie, Becky, and Kristin sit for hours in front of a blazing campfire on a hot summer day to create the perfect cover for this book. I owe a huge debt of gratitude to Mary Abel, a longtime friend and accomplished editor—this book would not have been possible were it not for your careful reading and critique. And heaps of gratitude to Thea Marx, who enchanted me with soulful stories about sisterhood and about the great and still-wild American West.

Finally, I'd like to thank my editor and Andrews McMeel editorial director, Chris Schillig, who believed in this book from the very first moment I proposed it to her.

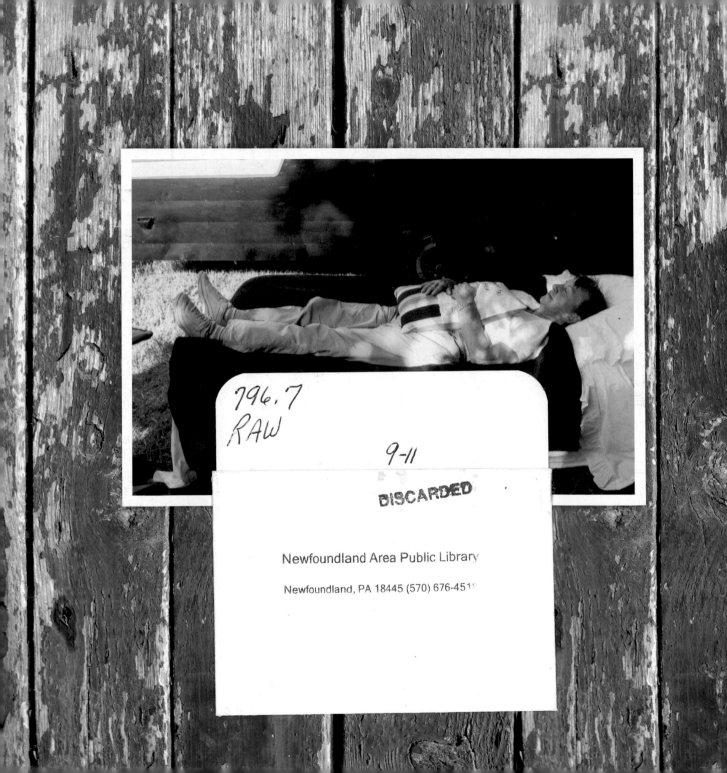